MW00454359

Praise for Michael E. Gerber, Dr. Donald L. Hayes, DC, and *The E-Myth Nutritionist*

I applaud Dr. Hayes for his collaborative effort with Michael Gerber, bringing together his expertise in nutrition with Gerber's E-Myth principles. My undergraduate work in biochemistry and nutrition, prior to my chiropractic journey, has always taught me the value of proper human biochemistry as a greater expression of health potential. **This amazing book is a must-read, not only to help you achieve greater practice success, but more importantly, to help you serve your people more effectively in this world's nutritional wasteland.**

Billy DeMoss, DC, DeMoss Chiropractic,
California Jam, DCS, *Spizz Magazine*

Dr. Hayes has been one of the most important teachers I have had the privilege to know in my 25-year clinical career. His ability to educate and inspire is second-to-none. I have been applying the principles of the E-Myth to my practice for over 20 years. This has allowed me to create one of the most successful non-insurance-based nutrition practices in the country. **Integrating Dr. Hayes' *Whole Body Alkaline Nutrition System* into your practice together with the E-Myth platform will allow you to help thousands of patients, improve your bottom line in this "post-insurance" era, and ensure that you make a difference in our healthcare system.**

Tom Bilella, DC, MS, CCN, CNS, DACBN, CISSN,
Nutrition Treatment Center, Red Bank, New Jersey

From practitioner to teacher to consultant to ultra-successful entrepreneur **Dr. Hayes is a systems-driven model of excellence who understands the business of nutrition at the deepest level**—there is no one better to demonstrate and communicate Michael Gerber's E-Myth principles for the nutrition practice.

Dennis Perman, DC, Co-Founder of The Masters Circle

Dr. Hayes' passion for health, healing, and nutrition is evident in every article he writes and every lecture he delivers. His uncomplicated approach to complex issues makes him a favorite at our teaching and training programs. **Don's business models and formulations offer solutions for the wellness practice, which in turn make a difference in communities around the world.**

Dr. David Fletcher DC, FRCCSS(C), Chairman, Creating Wellness
Systems and Chiropractic Leadership Alliance (CLA)

Dr. Hayes has explained, in an effective and easy-to-understand manner, how to combine his extraordinary nutritional expertise and background with the imperative E-Myth business principles. After spending 50 years starting and running a variety of businesses, I have found that one of the most important words for success is "Systems." Dr. Hayes has captured this essential business principle for the world of nutrition. Order out of chaos, at its best! A Must Read!"

Donald C. Hannah, Chairman Emeritus, Vital Living Inc.; Chairman Emeritus, Merrill
Lynch Realty Auction Division; Chairman & CEO, Hannah Marine Company

With the epidemic of obesity plaguing society today, this is a must-read book. Learn how acidity causes inflammation and how inflammation is the underlying cause of so much disease and suffering. **Reading this book is like reading an owner's manual for life.**

Dr. Bob Hoffman, President of The Masters Circle

Michael Gerber's *The E-Myth* is one of only four books I recommend as required reading. **For those looking to start and build a business of their own, this is the man who has coached more successful entrepreneurs than the next ten gurus combined.**

Timothy Ferris, #1 *New York Times* best-selling author, *The 4-Hour Workweek*

Everyone needs a mentor, someone who tells it like it is, holds you accountable, and shows you your good, bad, and ugly. For millions of small-business owners, Michael Gerber is that person. Let Michael be your mentor and you are in for a kick in the pants, the ride of a lifetime.

John Jantsch, author, *Duct Tape Marketing*

Michael Gerber's strategies in *The E-Myth* were instrumental in building my company from two employees to a global organization; I can't wait to see how applying the strategies from *Awakening the Entrepreneur Within* will affect its growth!

Dr. Ivan Misner, founder and chairman, BNI; author, *Masters of Sales*

Michael Gerber's gift to isolate the issues and present simple, direct, business-changing solutions shines bright with *Awakening the Entrepreneur Within*. If you're interested in developing an entrepreneurial vision and plan that inspires others to action, buy this book, read it, and apply the processes Gerber brilliantly defines.

Tim Templeton, author, *The Referral of a Lifetime*

Michael Gerber is a master instructor and a leader's leader. As a combat F-15 fighter pilot, I had to navigate complex missions with life-and-death consequences, but until I read *The E-Myth* and met Michael Gerber, my transition to the world of small business was a nightmare with no real flight plan. The hands-on, practical magic of Michael's turnkey systems magnified by the raw power of his keen insight and wisdom have changed my life forever.

Steve Olds, CEO, Stratworx.com

Michael Gerber truly, truly understands what it takes to be a successful practicing entrepreneur and business owner. He has demonstrated to me over six years of working with him that for those who stay the course and learn much more than just "how to work on their business and not in it," then they will reap rich rewards. I finally franchised my business, and the key to unlocking this kind of potential in any business is the teaching of Michael's work.

Chris Owen, marketing director, Royal Armouries (International) PLC

Michael's work has been an inspiration to us. **His books have helped us get free from the out-of-control life that we once had. His no-nonsense approach kept us focused on our ultimate aim rather than day-to-day stresses. He has helped take our business to levels we couldn't have imagined possible.** In the Dreaming Room™ made us totally re-evaluate how we thought about our business and our life. We have now redesigned our life so we can manifest the dreams we unearthed in Michael's Dreaming Room™.

Jo and Steve Davison, founders, The Spinal Health Clinic
Chiropractic Group and www.your-dream-life.com

Because of Michael Gerber, I transformed my twenty-four-hour-a-day, seven-day-a-week job (also called a small business) into a multimillion-dollar turnkey business. This in turn set the foundation for my worldwide training firm. **I am living my dream because of Michael Gerber.**

Howard Partridge, Phenomenal Products Inc.

Michael Gerber is an outrageous revolutionary who is changing the way the world does business. **He dares you to commit to your grandest dreams and then shows you how to make the impossible a reality. If you let him, this man will change your life.**

Fiona Fallon, founder, Divine and The Bottom Line

Michael Gerber is a genius. Every successful business person I meet has read Michael Gerber, refers to Michael Gerber, and lives by his words. You just can't get enough of Michael Gerber. **He has the innate (and rare) ability to tap into one's soul, look deeply, and tell you what you need to hear. And then, he inspires you and equips you with the tools to get it done.**

Pauline O'Malley, CEO, TheRevenueBuilder

When asked "Who was the most influential person in your life?" I am one of the thousands who don't hesitate to say "Michael E. Gerber." **Michael helped transform me from someone dreaming of retirement to someone dreaming of working until age one hundred.** This awakening is the predictable outcome of anyone reading Michael's new book.

Thomas O. Bardeen

Michael Gerber is an incredible business philosopher, guru, perhaps even a seer. He has an amazing intuition, which allows him to see in an instant what everybody else is missing; he sees opportunity everywhere. **While I was in the Dreaming Room™, Michael gave me the gift of seeing through the eyes of an awakened entrepreneur, and instantly my business changed from a regional success to serving clients on four continents.**

Keith G. Schiehl, president, Rent-a-Geek Computer Services

Michael Gerber is among the very few who truly understand entrepreneurship and small business. While others talk about these topics in the form of theories, methodologies, processes, and so on, Michael goes to the heart of the issues. **Whenever Michael writes about entrepreneurship, soak it in, as it is not only good for your business, but great for your soul.** His words will help you to keep your passion and balance while sailing through the uncertain sea of entrepreneurship.

Raymond Yeh, co-author, *The Art of Business*

Michael Gerber forced me to think big, think real, and gave me the support network to make it happen. A new wave of entrepreneurs is rising, much in thanks to his amazing efforts and very practical approach to doing business.

Christian Kessner, founder, Higher Ground Retreats and Events

Michael's understanding of entrepreneurship and small-business management has been a difference maker for countless businesses, including Infusion Software. **His insights into the entrepreneurial process of building a business are a must-read for every small-business owner.** The vision, clarity, and leadership that came out of our Dreaming Room™ experience were just what our company needed to recognize our potential and motivate the whole company to achieve it.

Clate Mask, president and CEO, Infusion Software

Michael Gerber is a truly remarkable man. His steady openness of mind and ability to get to the deeper level continue to be an inspiration and encouragement to me. **He seems to always ask that one question that forces the new perspective to break open, and he approaches the new coming method in a fearless way.**

Rabbi Levi Cunin, Chabad of Malibu

The Dreaming Room™ experience was literally life-changing for us. **Within months, we were able to start our foundation and make several television appearances owing to his teachings.** He has an incredible charisma, which is priceless, but above all Michael Gerber awakens passion from within, enabling you to take action with dramatic results . . . starting today!

Shona and Shaun Carcary
Trinity Property Investments Inc.—Home Vestors franchises

I thought *E-Myth* was an awkward name! What could this book do for me? **But when I finally got to reading it . . . it was what I was looking for all along.** Then, to top it off, I took a twenty-seven-hour trip to San Diego just to attend the Dreaming Room™, where Michael touched my heart, my mind, and my soul.

Helmi Natto, president, Eye 2 Eye Optics, Saudi Arabia

I attended In the Dreaming Room™ and was challenged by Michael Gerber to "Go out and do what's impossible." So I did; **I became an author and international speaker and used Michael's principles to create a world-class company that will change and save lives all over the world.**

Dr. Don Kennedy, MBA; author, *5 AM & Already Behind*, www.bahbits.com

I went to the Dreaming Room™ to have Michael Gerber fix my business. He talked about Dreaming. What was this Dreaming? I was too busy working! Too busy being miserable, angry, frustrated, behind in what I was trying to accomplish. And losing everything I was working for. **Then Michael Gerber woke up the dreamer in me and remade my life and my business.**

Pat Doorn, president, Mountain View Electric Ltd.

Michael Gerber can captivate a room full of entrepreneurs and take them to a place where they can focus on the essentials that are the underpinning of every successful business. He gently leads them from where they are to where they need to be in order to change the world.

Francine Hardaway, CEO, Stealthmode Partners
founder, the Arizona Entrepreneurship Conferences

The **E** Myth
Nutritionist

Why Most Healthcare Practices Don't Work and What to Do About It

MICHAEL E. GERBER
DONALD L. HAYES, DC

PRODIGY
BUSINESS BOOKS

Published by
Prodigy Business Books, Inc., Carlsbad, California.

Production Team
Patricia Beaulieu, COO, Prodigy Business Books, Inc.; Jenny Sommerfeld, editor;
Erich Broesel, cover designer, BroeselDesign, Inc.; Nancy Ratkiewich, book production,
njr productions; Jeff Kassebaum, Michael E. Gerber author photographer, Jeff
Kassebaum and Co.; Creative Images, San Clemente, CA, Dr. Donald L. Hayes, DC
co-author photographer.

For general information on other products and services, please visit the website:
www.michaelegerber.com.

ISBN 978-1-61835-029-9 (cloth)
ISBN 978-1-61835-031-2 (audio)
ISBN 978-1-61835-030-5 (e-book)

Printed in the United States of America

10 9 8 7 6 5 4 3 2 1

To Luz Delia, whose heart expands mine,
whose soul inspires mine,
whose boldness reaches for the stars, thank you,
forever, for being, truly mine . . .

—Michael E. Gerber

CONTENTS

A WORD ABOUT THIS BOOK

Michael E. Gerber

My first E-Myth book was published in 1985. It was called *The E-Myth: Why Most Businesses Don't Work and What to Do About It*. Since that book, and the company I created to provide business development services to its many readers, millions have read *The E-Myth* and the book that followed it, called *The E-Myth Revisited*, and tens of thousands have participated in our E-Myth Mastery programs.

The co-author of this book, Dr. Donald L. Hayes, DC, is one of my more enthusiastic readers, and through the implementation of E-Myth systems, his healthcare practice became an incredibly successful healthcare business.

This book is two things: the product of my lifelong work conceiving, developing, and growing the E-Myth way into a business model that has been applied to every imaginable kind of company in the world, as well as a product of Dr. Hayes' extraordinary experience and success applying the E-Myth to the development of his equally extraordinary enterprise.

So it was that one day, while sitting with my muse, which I think of as my inner voice, and which many who know me think of as "here he goes again!" I thought about the creation of an entire series of E-Myth Expert books. That series, including this book, would be co-authored by experts in every industry who had successfully applied my E-Myth principles to the extreme development of a practice—a very small company—with the intent of growing it nationwide, and even worldwide, which is what Dr. Hayes had in mind as he began to discover the almost infinite range of opportunities provided by thinking the E-Myth way.

Upon seeing the possibilities of this new idea, I immediately invited co-authors such as Dr. Hayes to join me. They said, "Let's do it!" and so we did.

Welcome to *The E-Myth Nutritionist: Why Most Healthcare Practices Don't Work and What to Do About It*.

Read it, enjoy it, and let us—Dr. Hayes and I—help you apply the E-Myth to the re-creation, development, and extreme growth of your practice into an enterprise that you can be justifiably proud of.

To your life, your wisdom, and the life and success of your clients, I wish you good reading.

—Michael E. Gerber
Co-Founder/Chairman
Michael E. Gerber Companies, Inc.
Carlsbad, California
www.michaelegerber.com/co-author

A NOTE FROM DR. HAYES

Dr. Donald L. Hayes, DC

I became a licensed chiropractor in 1977 and, as most new doctors did in those days, I went to work as an associate doctor to get some all-important experience on how to run a practice. I felt pretty confident about my technical skills as a chiropractor, but was smart enough to realize I didn't have the foggiest idea how to operate a chiropractic practice.

After about a year as an associate, I opened my own clinic in Salinas, California. My wife and I borrowed $10,000, threw open the doors, and hoped for the best. Things went well right from the start, primarily because the doctor whom I had worked for kept referring over all of his excess new patients. I thought I was doing pretty well, but not as well as I had imagined. While expressing my disappointment in slow growth to a doctor I went to school with, he suggested that I call and speak to a business consultant in the San Francisco Bay Area. I asked if this consultant was a chiropractor and he said no. I asked if he specialized in chiropractic practices and he again said no. I asked why in the world would I hire a business consultant who doesn't know as much as I do about chiropractic? He said, "Don, trust me and just call him." It took me a couple of weeks to make the call, but I finally decided I had nothing to lose.

To this day, I'm not sure if the man I spoke to on the other end of the phone was Michael E. Gerber or one of his associates, but I guess it doesn't matter. The man was polite and asked me several questions about my practice. I told him all the good things I could, tried my best to impress him, but it didn't seem to work. I remember the last question he asked me like it was yesterday.

"Dr. Hayes," he said, "if you and your wife hired an associate to run your practice and the two of you took an extended vacation, say for six months, would your practice income go down at all?"

"Go down!?" I remember saying. "My entire practice would go away!"

The man laughed and said, "Dr. Hayes, you don't have a business, you have a job. If you want to learn how to turn that job into a business, that's what our company does."

That man's last question to me, my honest response back, and his staggering reply not only blew my mind, it began my thirty-five-year relationship with Michael E. Gerber and his E-Myth principles—a relationship that has culminated in my having the privilege to co-author this book with my long-time mentor.

After meeting with Michael and applying his E-Myth principles, I went on from my single chiropractic practice in Salinas to open three additional practices, and operated all four of them for nearly twenty years using the principles of the E-Myth.

I began a second business, a management company to help other chiropractors use the E-Myth principles. I started my third business when I took my E-Myth skills to the owner and founder of the largest nutrition company in the world at that time and convinced him that the two of us should become business partners in a training program where I would teach his most successful doctors how to organize their nutrition profit centers around E-Myth systems.

And finally, I opened my fourth business, my own nutrition company where, along with my line of nutrition products, I teach my own clients a nutrition system based on the E-Myth protocols.

Although his wisdom helped me launch each of my successive businesses, I had never met Michael in person—and I had only heard him speak once to a live audience in all those thirty-five years. You can imagine what a rush it was when Michael E. Gerber himself scheduled a phone call with me to decide if he wanted to invite me to be his co-author on his newest book.

And so in May of 2012 I found myself driving to Carlsbad, California to have lunch with Michael and discuss the writing of this book. It was a dream come true to finally meet the man whose teachings had impacted everything I had done in business for the past thirty-five years, and to create this book to pass on my experience working with the the E-Myth.

The Need for *The E-Myth Nutritionist*

I told Michael that this book needed to be written. I told him it's more than just a business book—it's a health book that can help improve the lives of millions of people. The state of nutrition in our society today is horrific. Doctors who have all the necessary credentials and technical skills in the field of nutrition don't have a clue how to successfully offer nutrition inside of their regular practice. If we could help even a small percentage of healthcare practitioners successfully offer nutrition to their existing patient base, we could not only make their practices more successful, but much more importantly, we could substantially improve the health of the world. Michael agreed and this project was born.

The U.S. Department of Agriculture's Center for Nutrition Policy and Promotion compiled their Healthy Eating Index and found that only 10 percent of Americans have a good diet. The index was based on ten aspects of diet, including how many servings of fruits and vegetables were being consumed, along with how much sodium, cholesterol, and variety were present in the diet.

The USDA pointed out in the study that poor or inadequate diets are linked to four of the top ten causes of death, including heart disease, cancer, stroke, and diabetes. And the study concluded that most Americans have less-than-ideal diets that essentially leave their bodies starving for nutrients. Along with poor diets, studies have found that key nutrients in foods have declined from 1909 to 1994, likely because of two main factors: the soil is not as nutrient-dense as it once was, and the processing of foods degrades those nutrients that do exist. So not only are Americans eating fewer healthy foods, but those they do eat contain fewer nutrients than they once did.

If you're a healthcare practitioner who wants to maximize the well-being of patients while simultaneously improving the bottom line of your practice, this book is for you. Both of these concepts are equally important, because if you're not successful in practice, you may not stay in business in these tough economic times, and therefore you will not be around to provide better nutrition to the people who so desperately need it.

Here's to your health and success.

—Donald L. Hayes, DC
President & Owner
Wellness Watchers Global, LLC
Boca Raton, Florida

PREFACE

Michael E. Gerber

I am not a healthcare practitioner, though I have helped dozens of healthcare practitioners reinvent their practices over the past thirty-five years.

I like to think of myself as a thinker, maybe even a dreamer. Yes, I like to *do* things. But before I jump in and get my hands dirty, I prefer to think through what I'm going to do and figure out the best way to do it. I imagine the impossible, dream big, and then try to figure out how the impossible can become the possible. After that, it's about how to turn the possible into reality.

Over the years, I've made it my business to study how things work and how people work—specifically, how things and people work best together to produce optimum results. That means creating an organization that can do great things and achieve more than any other organization can.

This book is about how to produce the best results as a real-world healthcare practitioner in the development, expansion, and *liberation* of your practice. In the process, you will come to understand what the practice of healthcare—as a *business*—is, and what it isn't. If you keep focusing on what it isn't, you're destined for failure. But if you turn your sights on what it *is*, the tide will turn.

This book, intentionally small, is about big ideas. The topics we'll be discussing in this book are the very issues that healthcare practitioners face daily in their practice. You know what they are: money, management, patients, and many more. My aim is to help you begin the exciting process of totally transforming the way you do business. As such, I'm confident that *The E-Myth Nutritionist* could well be the most important book on the business of nutrition that you'll ever read.

Unlike other books on the market, my goal is not to tell you how to do the work you do. Instead, I want to share with you the E-Myth philosophy as a way to revolutionize the way you think about the work you do. I'm convinced that this new way of thinking is something healthcare practitioners everywhere must adopt in order for their practice to flourish during these trying times. I call it strategic thinking, as opposed to tactical thinking.

In strategic thinking, also called systems thinking, you, the healthcare practitioner, will begin to think about your entire practice—the broad scope of it—instead of focusing on its individual parts. You will begin to see the end game (perhaps for the first time) rather than just the day-to-day routine that's consuming you—the endless, draining work I call "doing it, doing it, doing it."

Understanding strategic thinking will enable you to create a practice that becomes a successful business, with the potential to flourish as an even more successful enterprise. But in order for you to accomplish this, your practice, your business, and certainly your enterprise must work *apart* from you instead of *because* of you.

The E-Myth philosophy says that a highly successful practice can grow into a highly successful business, which in turn can become the foundation for an inordinately successful enterprise that runs smoothly and efficiently *without* the healthcare practitioner having to be in the office for ten hours a day, six days a week.

So what is "The E-Myth," exactly? The E-Myth is short for the Entrepreneurial Myth, which says that most businesses fail to fulfill their potential because most people starting their own business are not entrepreneurs at all. They're actually what I call technicians suffering from an entrepreneurial seizure. When *technicians suffering from an entrepreneurial seizure* start a practice of their own, they almost always end up working themselves into a frenzy; their days are booked solid with appointments, one patient after another.

These healthcare practitioners are burning the candle at both ends, fueled by too much coffee and too little sleep, and most of the time, they can't even stop to think.

In short, the E-Myth says that most healthcare practitioners don't own a true business—most own a job. They're doing it, doing it, doing it, hoping like hell to get some time off, but never figuring out how to get their business to run without them. And if your business doesn't run well without you, what happens when you can't be in two places at once? Ultimately, your practice will fail.

There are a number of prestigious schools throughout the world dedicated to teaching the science of healthcare. The problem is they fail to teach the *business* of it. And because no one is being taught how to run a practice as a business, some healthcare practitioners find themselves having to close their doors every year. You could be a world-class expert in microbiology or food and nutrition sciences, but when it comes to building a successful business, all that specified knowledge matters exactly zilch.

The good news is that you don't have to be among the statistics of failure in the healthcare profession. The E-Myth philosophy I am about to share with you in this book has been successfully applied to thousands of practices just like yours with extraordinary results.

The key to transforming your practice—and your life—is to grasp the profound difference between going to work *on* your practice (systems thinker) and going to work *in* your practice (tactical thinker). In other words, it's the difference between going to work on your practice as an entrepreneur and going to work in your practice as a healthcare practitioner.

The two are not mutually exclusive. In fact, they are essential to each other. The problem with most practices is that the systems thinker—the entrepreneur—is completely absent. And so is the vision.

The E-Myth philosophy says that the key to transforming your practice into a successful enterprise is knowing how to transform yourself from successful technician into successful technician-manager-entrepreneur. In the process, everything you do in your practice will be transformed. The door is then open to turning it into the kind of practice it should be—a practice, a business, an enterprise of pure joy.

The E-Myth not only *can* work for you, it *will* work for you. In the process, it will give you an entirely new experience of your business and beyond.

To your future and your life. Good reading.

—Michael E. Gerber
Co-Founder/Chairman
Michael E. Gerber Companies, Inc.
Carlsbad, California
www.michaelegerber.com/co-author

ACKNOWLEDGMENTS

Michael E. Gerber

As always, and never to be forgotten, there are those who give of themselves to make my work possible.

To my dearest and most forgiving partner, wife, friend, and co-founder, Luz Delia Gerber, whose love and commitment takes me to places I would often not go unaccompanied. .

To Jenny Sommerfeld whose keen editorial eye helped to put the finishing touches on the final package.

Erich Broesel, our stand-alone graphic designer and otherwise visual genius who supported the creation of all things visual that will forever be all things Gerber, we thank you, deeply, for your continuous contribution of things both temporal and eternal.

To Trish Beaulieu, wow, you are splendid.

And to Nancy Ratkiewich, whose work has been essential for you who are reading this.

To those many, many dreamers, thinkers, storytellers, and leaders, whose travels with me in The Dreaming Room™ have given me life, breath, and pleasure unanticipated before we met. To those many participants in my life (you know who you are), thank you for taking me seriously, and joining me in this exhilarating quest.

And, of course, to my co-authors, all of you, your genius, wisdom, intelligence, and wit have supplied me with a grand view of the world, which would never have been the same without you.

Love to all.

ACKNOWLEDGMENTS

Dr. Donald L. Hayes, DC

I would like to express my deepest gratitude to all the health-care practitioners who work tirelessly to bring health and wellness to the public. It is my hope that this book will enable you to extend your nutritional services to more people throughout the world.

To Deonn Elizabeth McKinney Hayes, my beautiful and loving wife, the love of my life, my soul mate for this lifetime, all past lifetimes and forever more, mother of our only child, partner and loudest raving fan. I owe everything to you!

To Michael & Luz Delia Gerber, I can't thank you enough for sharing your message. It has played a part in everything that has unfolded in my life.

To my business partner Stuart Benson, your wisdom and kindness shine through everything you do. I'm clearly a better person for having you in my life.

To my business partner Ryan Benson—along with your lovely wife Dani and your amazing son Jack—you make working together so much fun. Thank you for your continuous commitment and support.

To Earnie Hayes, my youngest brother, you made those long road trips and lecture circuit series seem short and fun. You're the best and you mean the world to me.

To Dorene McKinney, my sister-in-law, thanks for always being so positive and working so hard.

To Hazel J. Hayes, my mother, the love that you constantly poured out to us, your children, was nothing that can ever be duplicated. I love and miss you so much!

To John W. Hayes, my oldest brother, and sister-in-law Cathy, thank you both for taking me into your home and setting the stage for the rest of my life and all the things I currently have.

To Lee & Bette McKinney, my in-laws, thank you for your daughter, for always being there for us, and living a life of unconditional love to show all of us how it's done.

To Courtney Hayes-Jurcheck, my beautiful, innate, and spirited daughter, you are the most important teacher I've ever had. Not only have you given me as a father everything I could ask for in a child, but then you top it all by giving me my beautiful grandboy!

To John M. Jurcheck, my son-in-law and father of my grandchildren, thank you for being such a loving husband and father. Thank you also for all your hard work in editing this book. I'm certain it would not be the book it is today without all your loving effort.

To my grandson, Oliver Beckett Hayes Jurcheck, the absolute love of my life. OBH, every day you teach me the meaning of life and keep me young! You help me slow down and realize why I'm here. I know you will continue to shine forever, and I want you to know that your grandpa "DanDa" is so very proud of you and will always be with you, now and forever.

INTRODUCTION

Michael E. Gerber

A s I write this book, the recession continues to take its toll on American businesses. Like any other industry, healthcare is not immune. Healthcare practitioners all over the country are watching as patients defer visits for adjustments, wellness care and supportive nutritional supplements. At a time when per capita disposable income is at an all-time low, many people are choosing not to spend their hard-earned money on healthcare services for themselves and even for their children. As a result, healthcare moves from the realm of necessity to luxury, and regrettably, healthy lifestyles and preventive care become an expendable concern while industry revenue takes a sizable dip into the red.

Faced with a struggling economy and fewer and fewer patients, many healthcare practitioners I've met are asking themselves, "Why did I ever become a healthcare practitioner in the first place?"

And it isn't just a money problem. After thirty-five years of working with small businesses, many of them healthcare practices, I'm convinced that the dissatisfaction experienced by countless practitioners is not just about money. To be frank, the recession doesn't deserve all the blame, either. While the financial crisis our country is facing certainly hasn't made things any better, the problem started long before the economy tanked. Let's dig a little deeper. Let's go back to school.

Can you remember that far back? Whichever university or college you attended, you probably had some great teachers who helped you become the fine practitioner you are. These schools excel at teaching the science of healthcare; they'll teach you everything you need to know about how biochemistry and physics relate to the way in which food works in the body. But what they *don't* teach is the consummate skill set needed to be a successful healthcare practitioner, and they certainly don't teach what it takes to build a successful practice.

Obviously, something is seriously wrong. The education that healthcare practitioners receive in school doesn't go far enough, deep enough, broad enough. Colleges don't teach you how to relate to the *enterprise* of healthcare or to the *business* of healthcare; they only teach you how to relate to the *practice* of healthcare. In other words, they merely teach you how to be an *effective* rather than a *successful* healthcare practitioner. Last time I checked, they weren't offering degrees in success. That's why most healthcare practitioners are effective, but few are successful.

Although a successful healthcare practitioner must be effective, an effective healthcare practitioner does not have to be—and in most cases isn't—successful.

An effective healthcare practitioner is capable of executing his or her duties with as much certainty and professionalism as possible.

A successful healthcare practitioner, on the other hand, works balanced hours, has little stress, leads rich and rewarding relationships with friends and family, and has an economic life that is diverse, fulfilling, and shows a continuous return on investment.

A successful healthcare practitioner finds time and ways to give back to the community but at little cost to his or her sense of ease.

A successful healthcare practitioner is a leader, not simply someone who teaches patients how to care for themselves and protect their health, but a sage; a rich person (in the broadest sense of the word); a strong father, mother, wife, or husband; a friend, teacher, mentor, and spiritually grounded human being; and a person who can see clearly into all aspects of what it means to lead a fulfilling life.

So let's go back to the original question. Why did you become a healthcare practitioner? Were you striving to just be an effective one, or did you dream about real and resounding success?

I don't know how you've answered that question in the past, but I am confident that once you understand the strategic thinking laid out in this book, you will answer it differently in the future.

If the ideas here are going to be of value to you, it's critical that you begin to look at yourself in a different, more productive way. I am suggesting that you go beyond the mere technical aspects of your daily job as a healthcare practitioner and begin instead to think strategically about your practice as both a business and an enterprise.

I often say that most *practices* don't work—the people who own them do. In other words, most practices are jobs for the healthcare practitioners who own them. Does this sound familiar? The healthcare practitioner, overcome by an entrepreneurial seizure, has started his or her own practice, become his or her own boss, and now works for a lunatic!

The result: the healthcare practitioner is running out of time, patience, and ultimately money. Not to mention paying the worst price anyone can pay for the inability to understand what a true practice is, what a true business is, and what a true enterprise is—the price of his or her life.

In this book I'm going to make the case for why you should think differently about what you do and why you do it. Dr. Hayes and I will show you not only why you should include nutrition in your practice, but also how to do it successfully. It isn't just the future of your practice that hangs in the balance. It's the future of your life.

The E-Myth Nutritionist is an exciting departure from my other sole-authored books. In this book, an expert—a Doctor of Chiropractic who has spent many years in the field of nutrition and has taught hundreds of fellow healthcare practitioners how to successfully use nutrition in their practice —is sharing his secrets about how to achieve extraordinary results using the E-Myth paradigm. In addition to the time-tested E-Myth strategies and systems I'll be sharing with you, you'll benefit from the wisdom, guidance, and practical tips provided by Dr. Hayes.

The problems that afflict healthcare practices today don't only exist in the field of healthcare; the same problems are confronting every organization of every size, in every industry in every country in the world. *The E-Myth Nutritionist* is next in a new series of E-Myth Expert books that will serve as a launching pad for Michael E. Gerber Partners™ to bring a legacy of expertise to small, struggling businesses in *all* industries. This series will offer an exciting opportunity to understand and apply the significance of E-Myth methodology in both theory and practice to businesses in need of development and growth.

The E-Myth says that only by conducting your business in a truly innovative and independent way will you ever realize the unmatched joy that comes from creating a truly independent business, a business that works *without* you rather than *because* of you.

The E-Myth says that it is only by learning the difference between the work of a *business* and the business of *work* that healthcare practitioners will be freed from the predictable and often overwhelming tyranny of the unprofitable, unproductive routine that consumes them on a daily basis.

The E-Myth says that what will make the ultimate difference between the success or failure of your healthcare practice that offers nutrition is first and foremost how you *think* about your business, as opposed to how hard you work in it.

So, let's think it through together. Let's think about those things—work, patients, money, time—that dominate the world of healthcare practitioners everywhere.

Let's talk about planning. About growth. About management. About getting a life!

Let's think about improving your and your family's life through the development of an extraordinary practice. About getting the life you've always dreamed of but never thought you could actually have.

Envision the future you want, and the future is yours.

CHAPTER

1

The Story of Steve and Peggy

Michael E. Gerber

You leave home to seek your fortune and, when you get it, you go home and share it with your family.

—Anita Baker

Every business is a family business. To ignore this truth is to court disaster.

This is true whether or not family members actually work in the business. Whatever their relationship with the business, every member of a healthcare practitioner's family will be greatly affected by the decisions a healthcare practitioner makes about the business. There's just no way around it.

Unfortunately, most healthcare practitioners tend to compartmentalize their lives. They view their practice as a profession—what they do—and therefore it's none of their family's business.

"This has nothing to do with you," says the healthcare practitioner to his wife, with blind conviction. "I leave work at the office and family at home."

1

And with equal conviction, I say, "Not true!"

In actuality, your family and practice are inextricably linked to one another. What's happening in your practice is also happening at home. Consider the following and ask yourself if each is true:

- If you're angry at work, you're also angry at home.
- If you're out of control in your practice, you're equally out of control at home.
- If you're having trouble with money in your practice, you're also having trouble with money at home.
- If you have communication problems in your practice, you're also having communication problems at home.
- If you don't trust in your practice, you don't trust at home.
- If you're secretive in your practice, you're equally secretive at home.

And you're paying a huge price for it!

The truth is that your practice and your family are one—and you're the link. Or you should be. Because if you try to keep your practice and your family apart, if your practice and your family are strangers, you will effectively create two separate worlds that can never wholeheartedly serve each other. Two worlds that split each other apart.

Let me tell you the story of Steve and Peggy Walsh.

The Walshes met in college. They were lab partners in organic chemistry, Steve a pre-chiropractic student and Peggy pre-nursing. When their lab discussions started to wander beyond spectroscopy and carboxylic acids and into their personal lives, they discovered they had a lot in common. By the end of the course, they weren't just talking in class; they were talking on the phone every night . . . and *not* about organic chemistry.

Steve thought Peggy was absolutely brilliant, and Peggy considered Steve the most passionate man she knew. It wasn't long before they were engaged and planning their future together. A week after graduation, they were married in a lovely garden ceremony in Peggy's childhood home.

While Steve studied at a prestigious college of chiropractic, Peggy entered a nursing program nearby. Over the next few years, the couple worked hard to keep their finances afloat. They worked long hours and studied constantly; they were often exhausted and struggled to make ends meet. But through it all, they were committed to what they were doing and to each other.

After passing his state boards, Steve became an associate doctor in a busy practice while Peggy began working in a large hospital nearby. Soon afterward, the couple had their first son, and Peggy decided to take some time off from the hospital to be with him. Those were good years. Steve and Peggy loved each other very much, were active members in their church, participated in community organizations, and spent quality time together. The Walshes considered themselves one of the most fortunate families they knew.

But work became troublesome. Steve grew increasingly frustrated with the way the practice was run and the fact that the senior doctor refused to consider offering nutrition as part of the patients' treatment programs. "I want to go into business for myself," he announced one night at the dinner table. "I want to start my own practice and offer nutrition when I choose.

Steve and Peggy spent many nights talking about the move. Was it something they could afford? Did Steve really have the skills necessary to make a chiropractic practice that offers nutrition a success? Were there enough patients to go around? What impact would such a move have on Peggy's career at the local hospital, their lifestyle, their son, their relationship? They asked all the questions they thought they needed to answer before Steve went into business for himself ... but they never really drew up a concrete plan.

Finally, tired of talking and confident that he could handle whatever he might face, Steve committed to starting his own practice. Additionally, he attended several post-graduate nutrition seminars and purchased a sizeable inventory of nutrition products from a few reputable manufacturers because he knew that most of his patients would benefit from them. Because she loved and supported him, Peggy agreed, offering her own commitment to help in any way she could. So Steve quit his job, took out a second mortgage on their home, and leased a small office nearby.

In the beginning, things went well. A building boom had hit the town, and new families were pouring into the area. Steve had no trouble getting new patients. His practice expanded, quickly outgrowing his office.

Within a year, Steve had employed an office manager, Clarissa, to run the front desk and handle the administrative side of the business. He also hired a bookkeeper, Tim, to handle the finances. Steve was ecstatic with the progress his young practice had made. He celebrated by taking his wife and son on vacation to Italy.

Of course, managing a business was more complicated and time-consuming than working for someone else. Steve not only supervised all the jobs Clarissa and Tim did, but also was continually looking for work to keep everyone busy. When he wasn't scanning journals of chiropractic to stay abreast of what was going on in the field or fulfilling continuing-education requirements to stay current on the standards of care, he was going to the bank, wading through patient paperwork, or speaking with insurance companies (which usually degenerated into *arguing* with insurance companies). He also found himself spending more and more time talking with his staff and patients about the benefits of using nutrition as part of the treatment plan, which seemed to take away from his time to deliver chiropractic adjustments. And he was spending a great deal of time on the telephone dealing with patient complaints and nurturing relationships.

As the months went by and more and more patients came through the door, Steve had to spend even more time just trying to keep his head above water.

By the end of its second year, the practice, now employing two full-time and two part-time people, had moved to a larger office downtown. The demands on Steve's time had grown with the practice.

He began leaving home earlier in the morning and returning later at night. He drank more. He rarely saw his son anymore. For the most part, Steve was resigned to the problem. He saw the hard work as essential to building the "sweat equity" he had long heard about.

Money was also becoming a problem for Steve. Although the practice was growing like crazy, money always seemed scarce when it was really needed. He had discovered that insurance companies were often slow to pay, and when they did, they cut his fee.

When Steve had worked for somebody else, he had been paid twice a month. In his own practice, he often had to wait—sometimes for months. He was still owed money on billings he had completed more than ninety days before.

When he complained to late-paying insurers, it fell on deaf ears. They would shrug, smile, and promise to do their best to review the claims, adding, "But your care plan does not meet medical necessity according to our guidelines." Of course, no matter how slowly Steve got paid, he still had to pay *his* people. This became a relentless problem. Steve often felt like a juggler dancing on a tightrope. A fire burned in his stomach day and night.

To make matters worse, Steve began to feel that Peggy was insensitive to his troubles. Not that he often talked to his wife about the practice. "Business is business" was Steve's mantra. "It's my responsibility to handle things at the office and Peggy's responsibility to take care of her own job and the family."

Peggy was working late hours at the hospital, and they'd brought in a nanny to help with their son. Steve couldn't help but notice that his wife seemed resentful, and her apparent lack of understanding baffled him. Didn't she see that he had a practice to take care of? That he was doing it all for his family? Apparently not.

As time went on, Steve became even more consumed and frustrated by his practice. When he went off on his own, he remembered saying, "I don't like people telling me what to do." But people were still telling him what to do. On one particularly frustrating morning, his office had to get an insurance authorization for a standard adjustment. It required a long-distance call and twenty-five minutes on hold. Steve was furious.

Not surprisingly, Peggy grew more frustrated by her husband's lack of communication. She cut back on her own hours at the hospital to focus on their family, but her husband still never seemed to be around. Their relationship grew tense and strained. The rare moments they *were* together were more often than not peppered by long silences—a far cry from the heartfelt conversations that had characterized their relationship's early days, when they'd talk into the wee hours of the morning.

Meanwhile, Tim, the bookkeeper, was also becoming a problem for Steve. Tim never seemed to have the financial information Steve needed to make decisions about payroll, patient billing, and general operating expenses, let alone how much money was available for Steve and Peggy's living expenses.

When questioned, Tim would shift his gaze to his feet and say, "Listen, Steve, I've got a lot more to do around here than you can imagine. It'll take a little more time. Just don't press me, okay?"

Overwhelmed by his own work, Steve usually backed off. The last thing Steve wanted was to upset Tim and have to do the books himself. He could also empathize with what Tim was going through, given the practice's growth over the past year.

Late at night in his office, Steve would sometimes recall his first years out of school. He missed the simple life he and his family had shared. Then, as quickly as the thoughts came, they would vanish. He had work to do and no time for daydreaming. "Having my own practice is a great thing," he would remind himself. "I simply have to apply myself, as I did in school, and get on with the job. I have to work as hard as I always have when something needed to get done."

Steve began to live most of his life inside his head. He began to distrust his people. They never seemed to work hard enough or to care about his practice as much as he did. If he wanted to go get something done, he usually had to do it himself. 8:27.15

Then one day, the office manager, Clarissa, quit in a huff, frustrated by the amount of work that her boss was demanding of her. Steve was left with a desk full of papers and a telephone that wouldn't stop ringing.

Clueless about the work Clarissa had done, Steve was overwhelmed by having to pick up the pieces of a job he didn't understand. His world turned upside down. He felt like a stranger in his own practice.

Why had he been such a fool? Why hadn't he taken the time to learn what Clarissa did in the office? Why had he waited until now?

Ever the trouper, Steve plowed into Clarissa's job with everything he could muster. What he found shocked him. Clarissa's work space was a disaster area! Her desk drawers were a jumble of papers, coins, pens, pencils, rubber bands, envelopes, business cards, fee slips, eye drops, and candy.

"What was she thinking?" Steve raged.

When he got home that night, even later than usual, he got into a shouting match with Peggy. He settled it by storming out of the house to get a drink. Didn't anybody understand him? Didn't anybody care what he was going through?

He returned home only when he was sure Peggy was asleep. He slept on the couch and left early in the morning, before anyone was awake. He was in no mood for questions or arguments.

When Steve got to his office the next morning, he immediately headed for the break room—maybe a cup of coffee could get rid of his throbbing headache.

What lessons can we draw from Steve and Peggy's story? I've said it once and I'll say it again: Every business is a family business. Your business profoundly touches all members of your family, even if they never set foot inside your office. Every business either gives to the family or takes from the family, just as individual family members do.

If the business takes more than it gives, the family is always the first to pay the price.

In order for Steve to free himself from the prison he created, he would first have to admit his vulnerability. He would have to confess to himself and his family that he really didn't know enough about his own practice and how to grow it.

Steve tried to do it all himself. Had he succeeded, had the practice supported his family in the style he imagined, he would have burst with pride. Instead, Steve unwittingly isolated himself, thereby achieving the exact opposite of what he sought.

He destroyed his life—and his family's life along with it.

Repeat after me: *Every business is a family business.*

Are you like Steve? I believe that all healthcare practitioners share a common soul with him. You must learn that a business is only a business. It is not your life. But it is also true that your business can have a profoundly negative impact on your life unless you learn how to do it differently than most healthcare practitioners do it—and definitely differently than Steve did it.

Steve's healthcare practice could have served his and his family's life. But for that to happen, he would have had to learn how to master his practice in a way that was completely foreign to him.

Instead, Steve's practice consumed him. Because he lacked a true understanding of the essential strategic thinking that would have allowed him to create something unique, Steve and his family were doomed from day one.

This book contains the secrets that Steve should have known. If you follow in Steve's footsteps, prepare to have your life and business fall apart. But if you apply the principles we'll discuss here, you can avoid a similar fate.

Let's start with the subject of *money*. But, before we do, let's learn the healthcare practitioner's view about the story I just told you. ✤

The Healthcare Practitioner's Nutrition Quest

Dr. Donald L. Hayes, DC

It is never too late to be who you might have been.

—George Eliot

The *American Heritage Medical Dictionary* defines a nutritionist as "a person who uses the science of nutrition to help individuals improve their health." It goes on to say that there is often no accreditation process for nutritionists, and those using the services of one should examine his or her qualifications carefully.

I have identified fourteen different health-related professions that often sell nutrition as part of their practice: nine that fall into the category of licensed healthcare practitioners and five that, although they are not doctors, may very well be licensed in their respective fields. I'm quite sure there are many more, it's simply difficult to know and list them all.

After practicing as a Doctor of Chiropractic for nearly twenty years, I agreed to a seven-year partnership with the owner and founder of the world's largest nutrition company at that time who formulated nutrition products exclusively for doctors. During this partnership, I had the exclusive privilege and great responsibility of training hundreds of doctors from all over the world, from nine distinct healthcare professions, on the use and application of hundreds of nutritional formulas. The doctors who attended my four-day nutrition boot camps came from the following fields:

- medicine
- chiropractic
- osteopathy
- naturopathy
- acupuncture
- homeopathy
- dentistry
- optometry
- podiatry

In addition, there were allied health personnel and staff who worked for these doctors and practiced as:

- registered dietitians
- athletic trainers
- kinesiologists
- licensed massage therapists
- personal trainers

This book is written not only for these fourteen different professions I've trained in the past, but also for the countless other fields of professional support that qualify as "the study of nutrition." I will, from time to time in my writings, weave in and out of the many different fields of nutrition.

Influenced by my professional career, my writings will no doubt seem to favor the chiropractic field, not because they have any exclusive right to nutrition, but because being one myself, I can't help but make reference to it. Please know that the information I provide is truly intended to help all who practice in this exciting field called nutrition.

Steve and Peggy Revisited

Michael's last chapter brings back a lot of memories for me. Many aspects of Steve and Peggy's story were part of my own personal experience in private practice before I made the switch from chiropractor to E-Myth entrepreneur (who happens to be practicing chiropractic). Through this transition, I learned early on that my practice was a family business and just how profoundly my practice, and how I operated it, affected my and my family's life. Without a doubt, the way my practice ran either contributed to, or detracted from, my family.

After nearly twenty years of operating four successful chiro- practic clinics using the E-Myth principles, I felt I was prepared to share my knowledge with the world. So when I was asked by the founder of that giant nutrition company to consult with his best doctor clients—who by all accounts ran some of the most successful nutrition profit centers in the world—I was excited, but also, I must admit, a bit intimidated.

Sure, I had my 400 hours of graduate-level nutrition education—like most chiropractors receive in their four-year curriculum—and I had practiced for nearly twenty years, but I was being asked to consult with doctors who were purchasing thousands of dollars worth of nutrition products every month and selling it (I assumed) quite successfully to their patients. What could they possibly learn from me? How could any of them be doing anything wrong?

My questions were answered as the E-Myth concept prevailed again! The E-Myth states that just because a person is loaded with the technical skills of a profession, it does not necessarily mean they know how to run a successful business that offers those technical skills. This proved true across the board, even with those seemingly successful practitioners. No matter their profession—medical, chiropractic, naturopathic, or otherwise—while they were all extremely competent in the clinical skills of nutrition, they nearly all failed when it came to the business of nutrition.

Were these doctors buying and selling a lot of nutrition products? Of course. Were these doctors helping to improve the health of their patients? Absolutely. Were these doctors making additional profits from all their work? Not really. Why not? Because without a nutrition system in place, I found that most of them were suffering from a concept that I call "trading dollars."

Trading Dollars

When a doctor suffers from the condition of "trading dollars," it means they spend so much time selling nutrition that they lose the equivalent amount of valuable clinical time that they could be using to provide their regular services. In other words, they may have made $10,000 a month selling nutrition, but by my estimation they lost $10,000 a month (or more!) by not being available to provide their regular healthcare services.

Doctors may love offering nutrition in their practice, but if all they manage to do is trade dollars, they don't have a business, they have a hobby—and a very expensive hobby at that. In my consultations, I found that the bigger the nutrition profit center, the more dollars were being traded.

To be clear, this was by no means a problem limited to these clients. Years later, after I left that partnership and formed my own company, I continued to consult doctors that were clients of all the major nutrition companies and found that, regardless of who they bought their nutrition products from, they all suffered from the same problem: a lack of nutrition business skills.

Mastering the Nutrition Profit Center

For the most part, doctors were never taught in school how to run and grow a nutrition business. Nutrition today is a multi-billion dollar, all-cash industry that doctors can tap into as much as they want, provided they understand and operate by the rules. If they don't, and continue to offer nutrition without any real system, they run the risk of trading dollars to the point that it could result in substantial financial loss.

Healthcare practitioners who choose to offer nutrition in their practice are doing so because they want to help their patients get better faster, not because they want to make more money. But the ironic thing is that if they don't use clear strategic thinking to develop a system that enables them to implement nutrition more effectively than most professionals do, then they are doomed to operate a practice that will never be as successful as it needs to be.

This book contains twenty-six chapters of business and life secrets that every healthcare practitioner who offers nutrition as part of their practice must understand and master to be successful.

Remember the old saying: "If you do what you've always done, you'll get what you've always gotten."

Make the changes necessary, apply the principles in this book to your profession, and experience the positive impact they can have on you, your practice, and your family. And with that, let's continue on to see what Michael has to share on the subject of money. ✿

CHAPTER 3

On the Subject
of Money

Michael E. Gerber

There are three faithful friends: an old wife, an old dog, and ready money.
—Benjamin Franklin

Had Steve and Peggy first considered the subject of *money* as
we will here, their lives could have been radically different.
Money is on the tip of every healthcare practitioner's
tongue, on the edge (or at the very center) of every healthcare practitioner's thoughts, intruding on every part of a healthcare practitioner's life.

With money consuming so much energy, why do so few healthcare practitioners handle it well? Why was Steve, like so many
healthcare practitioners, willing to entrust his financial affairs to a
relative stranger? Why is money scarce for most healthcare practitioners? Why is there less money than expected? And yet the demand
for money is always greater than anticipated.

What is it about money that is so elusive, so complicated, so difficult to control? Why is it that every healthcare practitioner I've ever

met hates to deal with the subject of money? Why are they almost always too late in facing money problems? And why are they constantly obsessed with the desire for more of it?

Money—you can't live with it and you can't live without it. But you'd better understand it and get your people to understand it. Because until you do, money problems will eat your practice for lunch.

You don't need an accountant or financial planner to do this. You simply need to prod your people to relate to money very personally. From the receptionist at the front counter to the technician, they all should understand the financial impact of what they do every day in relationship to the profit and loss of the practice.

And so you must teach your people to think like owners, not like technicians or office managers or receptionists. You must teach them to operate like personal profit centers, with a sense of how their work fits in with the practice as a whole.

You must involve everyone in the practice with the topic of money—how it works, where it goes, how much is left, and how much everybody gets at the end of the day. You also must teach them about the four kinds of money created by the practice.

The Four Kinds of Money

In the context of owning, operating, developing, and exiting from a healthcare practice, money can be split into four distinct but highly integrated categories:

- Income
- Profit
- Flow
- Equity

Failure to distinguish how the four kinds of money play out in your practice is a surefire recipe for disaster.

Important Note: Do not talk to your accountants or bookkeepers about what follows; it will only confuse them and you.

The information comes from the real-life experiences of thousands of small business owners, healthcare practitioners included, most of whom were hopelessly confused about money when I met them. Once they understood and accepted the following principles, they developed a clarity about money that could only be called enlightened.

The First Kind of Money: Income

Income is the money healthcare practitioners are paid by their practice for doing their job in the practice. It's what they get paid for going to work every day.

Clearly, if healthcare practitioners didn't do their job, others would have to, and they would be paid the money the practice currently pays the healthcare practitioners. Income, then, has nothing to do with ownership. Income is solely the province of *employeeship*.

That's why to the healthcare practitioners-as-*employee*, income is the most important form money can take. To the healthcare practitioner-as-*owner*, however, it is the least important form money can take.

Most important; least important. Do you see the conflict? The conflict between the healthcare practitioner-as-employee and the healthcare practitioner-as-owner?

We'll deal with this conflict later. For now, just know that it is potentially the most paralyzing conflict in a healthcare practitioner's life.

Failing to resolve this conflict will cripple you. Resolving it will set you free.

The Second Kind of Money: Profit

Profit is what's left over after a healthcare practice has done its job effectively and efficiently. If there is no profit, the practice is doing something wrong.

However, just because the practice shows a profit does not mean it is necessarily doing all the right things in the right way. Instead, it just means that something was done right during or preceding the period in which the profit was earned.

The important issue here is whether the profit was intentional or accidental. If it happened by accident (which most profit does), don't take credit for it. You'll live to regret your impertinence.

If it happened intentionally, take all the credit you want. You've earned it. Because profit created intentionally, rather than by accident, is replicable—again and again. And your practice's ability to repeat its performance is the most critical ability it can have.

As you'll soon see, the value of money is a function of your practice's ability to produce it in predictable amounts at an above-average return on investment.

Profit can be understood only in the context of your practice's purpose, as opposed to your purpose as a healthcare practitioner. Profit, then, fuels the forward motion of the practice that produces it. This is accomplished in four ways:

- Profit is *investment capital* that feeds and supports growth.
- Profit is *bonus capital* that rewards people for exceptional work.
- Profit is *operating capital* that shores up money shortfalls.
- Profit is *return-on-investment capital* that rewards you, the healthcare practitioner-owner, for taking risks

Without profit, a practice cannot subsist, much less grow. Profit is the fuel of progress.

If a practice misuses or abuses profit, however, the penalty is much like having no profit at all. Imagine the plight of a healthcare practitioner who has way too much return-on-investment capital and not enough investment capital, bonus capital, and operating capital. Can you see the imbalance this creates?

The Third Kind of Money: Flow

Flow is what money *does* in a healthcare practice, as opposed to what money *is*. Whether the practice is large or small, money tends to move erratically through it, much like a pinball. One minute it's there; the next minute it's not.

Flow can be even more critical to a practice's survival than profit, because a practice can produce a profit and still be short of money. Has this ever happened to you? It's called profit on paper rather than in fact.

No matter how large your practice, if the money isn't there when it's needed, you're threatened—regardless of how much profit you've made. You can borrow it, of course. But money acquired in dire circumstances is almost always the most expensive kind of money you can get.

Knowing where the money is and where it will be when you need it is a critically important task of both the healthcare practitioner-as-employee and the healthcare practitioner-as-owner.

Rules of Flow

You will learn no more important lesson than the huge impact flow can have on the health and survival of your healthcare practice, let alone your business or enterprise. The following two rules will help you understand why this subject is so critical.

1. **The First Rule of Flow states that your income statement is static, while the flow is dynamic.** Your income statement is a snapshot, while the flow is a moving picture. So, while your income statement is an excellent tool for analyzing your practice *after* the fact, it's a poor tool for managing it in the heat of the moment.

Your income statement tells you (1) how much money you're spending and where, and (2) how much money you're receiving and from where.

Flow gives you the same information as the income statement, plus it tells you *when* you're spending and receiving money. In other words, flow is an income statement moving through time. And that is the key to understanding flow. It is about management in real time. How much is coming in? How much is going out? You'd like to know this daily, or even by the hour if possible. Never by the week or month.

You must be able to forecast flow. You must have a flow plan that helps you gain a clear vision of the money that's out there next month and the month after that. You must also pinpoint what your needs will be in the future.

Ultimately, however, when it comes to flow, the action is always in the moment. It's about *now*. The minute you start to meander away from the present, you'll miss the boat.

Unfortunately, few healthcare practitioners pay any attention to flow until it dries up completely and slow pay becomes no pay. They are oblivious to this kind of detail until, say, patients announce that they won't pay for this or that. That gets a healthcare practitioner's attention because the expenses keep on coming.

When it comes to flow, most healthcare practitioners are flying by the proverbial seat of their pants. No matter how many people you hire to take care of your money, until you change the way you think about it, you will always be out of luck. No one can do this for you.

Managing flow takes attention to detail. But when flow is managed, your life takes on an incredible sheen. You're swimming with the current, not against it. You're in charge!

2. **The Second Rule of Flow states that money seldom moves as you expect it to.** But you do have the power to change that, provided you understand the two primary sources of money as it comes in and goes out of your healthcare practice.

The truth is, the more control you have over the *source* of money, the more control you have over its flow. The sources of money are both inside and outside your practice.

Money comes from *outside* your practice in the form of receivables, reimbursements, investments, and loans.

Money comes from *inside* your practice in the form of payables, taxes, capital investments, and payroll. These are the costs associated with attracting patients, delivering your services, operations, and so forth.

Few healthcare practitioners see the money going *out* of their practice as a source of money, but it is.

When considering how to spend money in your practice, you can save—and therefore make—money in three ways:

- Do it more effectively.
- Do it more efficiently.
- Stop doing it altogether.

By identifying the money sources inside and outside your practice, and then applying these methods, you will be immeasurably better at controlling the flow in your practice.

But what are these sources? They include how you

- manage your services;
- buy supplies and equipment;
- compensate your people;
- plan people's use of time;
- determine the direct cost of your services;
- increase the number of patients seen;
- manage your work;
- collect reimbursements and receivables; and
- countless more.

In fact, every task performed in your practice (and ones you haven't yet learned how to perform) can be done more efficiently and effectively, dramatically reducing the cost of doing business. In the process, you will create more income, produce more profit, and balance the flow.

The Fourth Kind of Money: Equity

Sadly, few healthcare practitioners fully appreciate the value of equity in their practice. Yet equity is the second most valuable asset any healthcare practitioner will ever possess. (The first most valuable asset is, of course, your life. More on that later.)

Equity is the financial value placed on your practice by a prospective buyer.

Thus, your *practice* is your most important product, not your services. Because your practice has the power to set you free. That's right. Once you sell your practice—providing you get what you want for it—you're free!

Of course, to enhance your equity, to increase your practice's value, you have to build it right. You have to build a practice that works. A practice that can become a true business and a business that can become a true enterprise. A practice/business/enterprise that can produce income, profit, flow, and equity better than any other healthcare practitioner's practice can.

To accomplish that, your practice must be designed so that it can do what it does systematically and predictably, every single time.

The Story of McDonald's

Let me tell you the most unlikely story anyone has ever told you about the successful building of a practice, business, and enterprise. Let me tell you the story of Ray Kroc.

You might be thinking, "What on earth does a hamburger stand have to do with my practice? I'm not in the hamburger business; I'm a healthcare practitioner."

Yes, you are. But by practicing healthcare as you have been taught, you've abandoned any chance to expand your reach, help more patients, or improve your services the way they must be improved if the practice of healthcare—and your life—is going to be transformed.

In Ray Kroc's story lies the answer.

Kroc called his first McDonald's restaurant "a little money machine." That's why thousands of franchises bought it. And the reason it worked? Kroc demanded consistency, so that a hamburger in Philadelphia would be an advertisement for one in Peoria. In fact, no matter where you bought a McDonald's hamburger in the 1950s, the meat patty was guaranteed to weigh exactly 1.6 ounces, with a diameter of 3⅝ inches. It was in the McDonald's handbook.

Did Kroc succeed? You know he did! And so can you, once you understand his methods. Consider just one part of his story.

In 1954, Kroc made his living selling the five-spindle Multimixer milkshake machine. He heard about a hamburger stand in San Bernardino, California, that had eight of his machines in operation, meaning it could make forty shakes simultaneously. This he had to see.

Kroc flew from Chicago to Los Angeles, then drove sixty miles to San Bernardino. As he sat in his car outside Mac and Dick McDonald's restaurant, he watched as lunch customers lined up for bags of hamburgers.

In a revealing moment, Kroc approached a strawberry blonde in a yellow convertible. As he later described it, "It was not her sex appeal but the obvious relish with which she devoured the hamburger that made my pulse begin to hammer with excitement."

Passion.

In fact, it was the french fry that truly captured his heart. Before the 1950s, it was almost impossible to buy fries of consistent quality. Kroc changed all that. "The french fry," he once wrote, "would become almost sacrosanct for me, its preparation a ritual to be followed religiously."

Passion and preparation.

The potatoes had to be just so—top-quality Idaho russets, 8 ounces apiece, deep-fried to a golden brown, and salted with a shaker that, as Kroc put it, kept going "like a Salvation Army girl's tambourine."

As Kroc soon learned, potatoes too high in water content—even top-quality Idaho russets varied greatly in water content—will come out soggy when fried. And so Kroc sent out teams of workers, armed with hydrometers, to make sure all his suppliers were producing potatoes in the optimal solids range of 20 percent to 23 percent.

Preparation and passion. Passion and preparation. Look those words up in the dictionary and you'll see Kroc's picture. Can you envision your picture there?

Do you understand what Kroc did? Do you see why he was able to sell thousands of franchises? Kroc knew the true value of equity, and, unlike Steve from our story, Kroc went to work *on* his business rather than *in* his business. He knew the hamburger wasn't his product—McDonald's was!

So what does *your* practice need to do to become a little money machine? What is the passion that will drive you to build a practice that works—a turnkey system like Ray Kroc's?

Equity and the Turnkey System

What's a turnkey system? And why is it so valuable to you? To better understand it, let's look at another example of a turnkey system that worked to perfection: the recordings of Frank Sinatra.

Frank Sinatra's records were to him as McDonald's restaurants were to Ray Kroc. They were part of a turnkey system that allowed Sinatra to sing to millions of people without having to be there himself.

Sinatra's recordings were a dependable turnkey system that worked predictably, systematically, automatically, and effortlessly to produce the same results every single time—no matter where they were played, and no matter who was listening.

Regardless of where Frank Sinatra was, his records just kept on producing income, profit, flow, and equity, over and over … and still do! Sinatra needed only to produce the prototype recording, and the system did the rest.

Kroc's McDonald's is another prototypical turnkey solution, addressing everything McDonald's needs to do in a basic, systematic way so that anyone properly trained by McDonald's can successfully reproduce the same results.

And this is where you'll realize your equity opportunity: in the way your practice does business, in the way your practice systematically does what you intend it to do, and in the development of your turnkey system—a system that works even in the hands of ordinary people (and healthcare practitioners less experienced than you) to produce extraordinary results.

Remember:

- If you want to build vast equity in your practice, then go to work *on* your practice, building it into a business that works every single time.
- Go to work *on* your practice to build a totally integrated turnkey system that delivers exactly what you promised every single time.
- Go to work *on* your practice to package it and make it stand out from the healthcare practices you see everywhere else.

Here is the most important idea you will ever hear about your practice and what it can potentially provide for you:

The value of your equity is directly proportional to how well your practice works. And how well your practice works is directly proportional to the effectiveness of the systems you have put into place upon which the operation of your practice depends.

Whether money takes the form of income, profit, flow, or equity, the amount of it—and how much of it stays with you—invariably boils down to this. Money, happiness, life—it all depends on how well your practice works. Not on your people, not on you, but on the system.

Your practice holds the secret to more money. Are you ready to learn how to find it?

Earlier in this chapter, I alerted you to the inevitable conflict between the healthcare practitioner-as-employee and the healthcare practitioner-as-owner. It's a battle between the part of you working *in* the practice and the part of you working *on* the practice. Between the part of you working for income and the part of you working for equity.

Here's how to resolve this conflict:

- Be honest with yourself about whether you're filling *employee* shoes or *owner* shoes.
- As your practice's key employee, determine the most effective way to do the job you're doing, *and then document that job.*

- Once you've documented the job, create a strategy for replacing yourself with someone else (another healthcare practitioner who understands the nutritional protocols) who will then use your documented system exactly as you do.
- Have your new employees manage the newly delegated system. Improve the system by quantifying its effectiveness over time.
- Repeat this process throughout your practice wherever you catch yourself acting as employee rather than owner.
- Learn to distinguish between ownership work and employee-ship work every step of the way.

Master these methods, understand the difference between the four kinds of money, develop an interest in how money works in your practice . . . and then watch it flow in with the speed and efficiency of a perfectly delivered adjustment.

Now let's take another step in our strategic thinking process. Let's look at the subject of *planning*. But first, let's see what Dr. Hayes has to say about money. ✤

4

Recurring Money From Nutrition

Dr. Donald L. Hayes, DC

Making money isn't hard in itself . . . What's hard is to earn it doing something worth devoting one's life to.

—Carlos Ruiz Zafon

Michael jumped into this book with both feet in the last chapter, tackling one of the most difficult subjects first, the one all healthcare practitioners have the most trouble with—money! Let's face it, we doctors do nothing but complain about our money problems. We certainly find people to blame, typically the insurance companies and managed care organizations, but when it comes down to fixing our money problems, we throw our hands in the air and basically do nothing.

That's no longer acceptable. Michael has laid out a blueprint of exactly what needs to be done in terms of money. You need to re-read his last chapter so many times that you can repeat it from memory.

I'm going to follow Michael's lead and say that, in addition to his advice, you must also do one other major thing in order to stop your money worries: either add a recurring nutrition revenue system (if you don't already have one), or change the one you have if it's not producing significant monthly residual income.

How can I be so confident that a systematized nutrition program will end all of your money worries? Take a look at the statistics below and I'm sure you'll agree that properly executed nutrition can increase your Income, Profit, Flow, and Equity.

Nutrition Will Grow Your Practice

In case you have any doubts about the positive financial impact that offering nutrition will have on your practice, let me share some statistics. Since I'm a chiropractor, I'm going to compare current nutrition industry sales with current chiropractic industry sales.

Since 1971, IBISWorld has been providing business leaders with thoroughly researched, accurate, and up-to-date business information. Their team of expert analysts gather and publish economic data which provides valuable insight into over 700 industries and helps business leaders make better business decisions. What follows are two market research reports compiled by IBISWorld that compare the chiropractic industry to the vitamin and supplement industry.

Chiropractors in the US: Market Research Report - $13 Billion

Chiropractic care has recently gained more legitimacy and greater acceptance among medical physicians and insurance practitioners. The chiropractic industry is in a mature phase with growth decelerating in recent years.

The value that the chiropractic industry adds to the overall US economy is expected to increase at an average annual rate of 0.8 percent from 2007 to 2017. Current revenues are estimated at $13 billion.

Vitamins and Supplements in the US: Market Research Report - $35 Billion

Although vitamins and supplements are often considered non-discretionary purchases, the industry has grown at a steady clip over the past five years due to several factors, including an aging population, reduced levels of employed and insured Americans, and increased consumer concerns toward health. Vitamins are taken to proactively maintain and improve health and to support specific health conditions. These products help prevent nutrient deficiencies that can occur when diet alone does not provide all the necessary vitamins.

Growth is forecast to continue, especially as disposable incomes recover. Through the recession, the industry managed to grow on the back of decreased access to health insurance, which led consumers to purchase vitamins and supplements as alternatives to expensive prescription drugs. A trend of health-consciousness also fueled demand for industry products.

The value that the vitamin and supplement industry adds to the overall US economy is forecast to increase at an average annual rate of 2.5 percent from 2007 to 2017. Current revenues are estimated at $29 billion in traditional sales and $6 billion in online sales for a total of $35 billion.

Patients Will Buy Nutrition from Their Healthcare Practitioner

Patients are coming to healthcare practitioners because they are sick and tired of being sick and tired. They wouldn't have made an appointment with an alternative practitioner, especially one that offers nutrition, if they weren't looking for an alternative to conventional healthcare.

Of course they want to know if nutrition combined with your treatments—be they chiropractic, acupuncture, massage therapy, etc.—will provide them the natural relief they want. Patients aren't concerned about price; they're not looking for the best deal in town. They know they're in the office of a professional and that the services and products professionals provide will cost money.

All you need to do is the right thing. Evaluate them the way you were taught in school, and make your recommendations. It's that simple! Always recommend the absolute best type of care. Always include all the services and products you know will help them resolve their condition in the shortest amount of time, including the purchase and use of nutrition supplements.

Add a Nutrition Profit Center Now

Based on the market data, healthcare practitioners need to add a nutrition profit center to their practice as soon as possible. In terms of the chiropractic profession, vitamin and supplement revenues at $35 billion are 2.6 times higher than chiropractic revenues at $13 billion. The predicted growth rate over the next ten years is 320 percent higher for vitamins and supplements (at 2.5 percent) than it is for chiropractic services (at only 0.8 percent).

Clearly, nutrition can offset all the losses that healthcare practitioners are experiencing due to the changing insurance reimbursement market. When doctors use nutrition as part of their regular treatment protocols to provide faster and more complete relief and recovery, patients will benefit tremendously, and will be more likely to return for care and re-purchase nutrition supplements.

Nutrition Will Increase All Four Kinds of Money

Michael told us in the last chapter about the four kinds of money we'll experience in practice:

1. Income, which is the owner's salary.
2. Profit, which is what's left over after paying bills.
3. Flow, which is how money travels around in your practice.
4. Equity, which is the amount of money a potential buyer thinks your practice is worth.

Michael also made it perfectly clear that the fourth kind, Equity, is the most important form of money and the biggest asset you have—even more important than you, your staff, and your services.

I know I can't speak for all healthcare practitioners, but in general if I tell a chiropractor they need to increase the value of their practice so it will build up their Equity, they'll look at me with a blank stare. "How do I do that?" they'll ask me. "What am I supposed to do? Work harder, hire more staff, do more weekend spinal screenings? What?"

Chiropractors don't think of Equity in their practice because most of them never think about selling it. They've never been told that if they establish a practice that has incredible value, they will be able to sell it someday to another chiropractor and walk away with a lot of cash. It's certainly not taught that way in chiropractic college, and typically never mentioned by accountants. This is a radical concept, one that takes the business knowledge and boldness of Michael to bring it to light.

Set a Nutrition Profit Center Money Goal

This might be a surprise to you, but offering nutrition in your practice is as much about learning who you are and who you want to be as a person as it is about the nutrition profit center itself. With that in mind, one of the first things you need to do is crystallize where you want to go with your nutrition profit center. Write down the goals for your nutrition profit center and be very clear on your money goals. If you don't set any goals or establish specific plans, then don't be surprised when your practice lacks direction or organization and a general panic develops, clouding the intention of your nutrition profit center.

I will elaborate on writing out specific plans later, but for now let's discuss setting a practice money goal that will increase all four kinds of money. Let's say you would like your nutrition profit center to generate enough recurring monthly revenue to pay all of your monthly practice overhead, including a reasonable monthly salary for yourself. Every doctor with whom I have ever consulted had exceptional knowledge and technical skills in the field of nutrition, but very few generated any substantial amount of recurring monthly revenue selling it. Why?

The E-Myth as it relates to the field of nutrition is the belief that any healthcare practitioner who starts a nutrition profit center is an entrepreneur. The problems begin because the doctor, who may have a lot of technical skills in the field of nutrition, knows nothing about setting up a system to run the nutrition business. After the initial exhilaration of the startup—that usually includes the purchase of a substantial amount of supplements—most doctors quickly become exhausted and demoralized when they find out that the products simply don't seem to sell very easily. Knowing nutrition inside and out has not prepared them to run a nutrition business. In fact, it ends up becoming a liability due to the misguided assumption that knowing a lot about nutrition would make selling it easy.

It does not have to be this way if you set up a nutrition system that runs the nutrition profit center. Most doctors believe that one of the best ways to grow their nutrition profit center is by hiring brilliant staff members. In fact, Gerber suggests that this is a "hit and miss" way of doing things. What doctors really need are nutritional turnkey systems and procedures that enable merely good staff to do extraordinary things; ways of operating the nutrition profit center that guarantee patient satisfaction not from individual staff members, but from within the system itself. If you can build a great nutrition profit center around an ordinary staff, you don't have to worry about finding an extraordinary one.

You can increase all four types of money—Income, Profit, Flow, and Equity—all at the same time if you use a Whole Body Alkaline Nutrition System in your existing practice and promote it to your patient base and the community at large.

Before I explain what Whole Body Alkaline Nutrition is, let me illustrate what it is not. If you're a healthcare practitioner offering nutrition in your practice today, you're probably doing it like every other doctor. The common thing doctors do wrong when it comes to offering nutrition is that they practice nutrition the same way they were taught to practice healthcare, a concept I call "Condition Specific Nutrition."

Condition Specific Nutrition

"Condition Specific Nutrition" is a term I coined during my consulting years. Condition Specific Nutrition isn't bad, and the term is certainly not meant to be derogatory in any way. It's simply the result of my seven years of observing hundreds of doctors who practice nutrition.

Condition Specific Nutrition is used when doctors choose to focus on a "local" issue that might benefit from better nutrition, instead of focusing on the big picture, or the "global" issues, that nutrition could help improve.

In my opinion, this type of nutrition does not do the most good for the patient and is a financial nightmare for the healthcare practitioner because it's too expensive and does not produce a recurring income stream for the practice.

Most healthcare practitioners who use the Condition Specific Nutrition model don't realize they are positioning their nutrition as a short-term fix as opposed to a lifestyle change where the patient may benefit from the nutritional supplements long-term.

Condition Specific Nutrition is typically a "this for that" concept: a patient sees the doctor for "this" condition, and the doctor recommends "that" particular supplement. Even though this seems perfectly logical from the doctor's point of view, patients see it differently. Patients, who are conditioned by the medical-pharmaceutical world, think the same way about supplements as they do about prescription drugs: when their symptoms subside, they stop taking the drug or the supplement. Most doctors who recommend nutrition intend for the patient to continue using the supplement long-term for their ongoing health benefit, but the doctor's message and protocols scream short-term use.

Another huge problem with using Condition Specific Nutrition's "this-for that" approach is that many of the supplements that are typically recommended with this type of system are isolated nutrients that can be purchased almost anywhere. When doctors recommend individual nutrition supplements (like multi-vitamins) and isolated nutrients (like glucosamine), patients will typically shop around for them. Since the internet is loaded with similar looking (but often poor quality) nutrition products at lower costs, we healthcare practitioners should not be surprised when patients take the recommendations we give them and purchase seemingly comparable but "cheaper" products elsewhere.

More Problems with Condition Specific Nutrition

Doctors that practice Condition Specific Nutrition typically have very high practice overheads. They have a lot of their cash tied up in the inventory of dozens, and possibly hundreds, of products. This requires extra staff to not only order and stock the products, but also to explain the products to patients. Furthermore, there is the unexpected cost of waste due to expiration of products on shelves and returns of half used bottles. And worst of all, these doctors are required to use too much of their precious clinic time to decide what to recommend because of all the different nutrition product options.

In terms of the four kinds of money, I have found that the doctors who practice Condition Specific Nutrition typically have lower Incomes, less Profit, poor Flow, and don't build additional Equity in their practice.

In fact, when it's all added up, overhead typically exceeds profits! Rarely do doctors make money, or have a chance to break even, using Condition Specific Nutrition. So very little, if any, recurring income occurs from this type of nutrition system. In the end, the Condition Specific Nutrition "this-for that" model is simply not worth it.

Whole Body Alkaline Nutrition

"Whole Body Alkaline Nutrition" is another term I coined, this time to identify a model of offering nutrition in a professional setting that provides patients with broad-based nutritional support. It's basically an umbrella approach to nutrition that will benefit all patients, regardless of their presenting complaints.

I developed the idea of Whole Body Alkaline Nutrition to combat my frustration with the growing complexity of the field. Over the past sixty years, nutrition has become extremely complicated in response to the growing pharmaceutical market. For instance, in 1950 there were about 5,000 prescription drugs on the market. Today that number has risen to over 50,000, evolving into a much more complicated field.

Similarly, in 1950 it was generally agreed that to be healthy from a nutritional perspective, a person needed only to consume forty essential micronutrients on a daily basis. These nutrients could typically be derived from eating a healthy diet and taking one or two high-quality nutritional supplements.

Today, new combinations of supplements appear every month to the point where the forty micronutrients have grown to 600-to-800 different supplements, creating a complex arena that confuses doctors and consumers alike. These days, it's routine for a health-care practitioner to be deluged with dozens of new supplements, while having to deal with nutrition catalogues that are hundreds of pages long.

Why the expansive growth of both the pharmaceutical and nutraceutical markets? One could say that with progress comes new and necessary drugs and nutrients, and one might also speculate that it's very good business for the manufacturers. I'll leave that decision up to you, dear reader, and instead share a bit more on the subject of Whole Body Alkaline Nutrition.

Benefits of Whole Body Alkaline Nutrition

Whole Body Alkaline Nutrition provides a plethora of major benefits to both the patient and the healthcare practitioner. I'll start with the more important of the two, the patient. Let's face it, every patient who enters your practice is suffering from some form of acute and/or chronic inflammation, regardless of their main complaint. The goal of Whole Body Alkaline Nutrition is to provide every patient with broad-based nutritional support that focuses on helping his or her body maintain homeostasis (or "balance"), as well as support a healthy inflammatory response, in the midst of any type of health challenge.

Whole Body Alkaline Nutrition, used in conjunction with your regular treatments, should speed up the rate of healing and shorten recovery times. Whole Body Alkaline Nutrition supplements that best support homeostasis and a healthy inflammatory response are those that alkalize the body and help it stay pH balanced. In addition, Whole Body Alkaline Nutrition should help to reduce overall systemic inflammation and target the five major types of free radicals. Common indicators of inflammation, such as C-Reactive Protein, erythrocyte sedimentation rate, and fibrinogen, should demonstrate noticeable reductions in their values with appropriate nutrition use. Whole Body Alkaline Nutrition should also help promote healthy weight management and protect the patient against micronutrient deficiency. This broad approach to nutrition should additionally help to facilitate proper muscle function and assist in the repair of connective tissue.

Whole Body Alkaline Nutrition is an "inside-outside" approach to reducing inflammation. By that I mean that the recommended nutrition products help to reduce the inflammation on the inside while the doctor provides their treatment—chiropractic, acupuncture, or other body work—on the outside.

The Science of Whole Body Alkaline Nutrition

Whole Body Alkaline Nutrition supplements that are alkalizing, pH balancing, anti-inflammatory, and nutrient-dense, are best delivered as powdered fruit and vegetable concentrates that mix easily and taste good in pure water. Patients should begin using these types of supplements on their first visit, when they are typically most inflamed. In most cases, having both an AM product that patients take first thing in the morning and a PM product that they take before going to bed will provide the most benefit because the body processes acid wastes while we sleep.

The powdered supplements should contain a full spectrum of high quality, nutrient-dense, dark green and brightly colored superfoods, and should demonstrate on Certificate of Analysis a very high Total ORAC Food and Nutrition Assay value for their antioxidant power against the five major types of free radicals. Finally, the products should be quick for doctors to recommend, easy for doctors and staff to explain, and extremely simple for anyone in the practice to administer.

Patients will feel the difference using Whole Body Alkaline Nutrition products, and because of that, many will choose to re-purchase them on a monthly basis. To make nutrition profitable in your office, supplements must be repurchased by a majority of patients on a monthly basis without any doctor or staff involvement. Just like consumers who go to their local health food store every month to buy their vitamins, if patients enjoy the product you provide and feel the difference, they will come to your office and do the same thing.

The Compounding Revenue Model for Whole Body Alkaline Nutrition

Compounding is a phenomenon that most of us don't fully understand or appreciate. MSN made a "person on the street" video where they asked several people if they would rather have $1 million dollars now or take a penny now and double it every day for thirty days. As you might expect, 90 percent of people chose to take the $1 million dollars right away. But it turns out that this is the less lucrative option because, with the power of compounding over thirty days, that single penny will become more than $5 million dollars by the end of the month. Clearly, the simple act of doubling your previous day's investment can rapidly reap huge rewards.

Selling one-to-two bottles of vitamins to patients in a Condition Specific type of practice can end up costing you more than it's worth because patients usually don't re-purchase their nutrition products. However, when Whole Body Alkaline Nutrition is part of your initial new patient protocols, you'll find more often than not that patients will continue to buy the product from you month after month.

The simple fact is that if you harness the power of compounding in your nutrition profit center, you can build a lot of Equity. When you offer a line of high quality Whole Body Alkaline Nutrition supplements that are linked to your practice principles of alkalizing the body, raising pH, reducing inflammation, and promoting healthy weight management, and then you offer these supplements consistently for two years, you will begin to experience the benefits of compounding. With a Whole Body Alkaline Nutrition approach, you make a few hundred dollars the first month, then you add an additional few hundred dollars each month, and at the end of two years you'll find that you've not only gained an additional revenue stream of $50,000-to-$100,000 a year or more, you've also built a real all-cash repeat business that will last.

Here's an example: Say your Whole Body Alkaline Nutrition supplements cost patients about $85 per month, which provides both day and night alkaline protection for one person for thirty days. These supplements (which, keep in mind, provide the anti-oxidant equivalent of fifteen or more servings of organic fruits and vegetables) cost your patients just $2.83 a day, or less than a medium latte at Starbucks. Through the magic of compounding, if you put just fifteen patients a month on the products, you'll generate tens of thousands of dollars of additional revenue. And remember, fifteen new people buying your products every month begins with just five-to-ten patients who enjoy the products. These patients will purchase additional products for their family and share how they feel with co-workers and friends who, in many cases, will also start purchasing nutrition from you.

When to Use Condition Specific Nutrition

Healthcare practitioners who implement Whole Body Alkaline Nutrition as a first line therapy can still consider recommending specific targeted products to those patients who they determine may need additional support.

Most doctors that I've advised stock between two-to-four different brands of nutrition products. With that in mind, a doctor could still stock a few favorite products that their experience shows will be needed by some patients, but at least they will not find themselves having to inventory the hundreds of products that are required when practicing Condition Specific Nutrition. Whole Body Alkaline Nutrition will deliver the most good, to the most patients, in the shortest amount of time, at the least cost to both the doctor and the patient—period!

Six Key Ways to Use Nutrition to Build Equity in Your Practice

1. Use a Whole Body Alkaline Nutrition system in your practice so you can offer support nutrition to every patient on their very first visit.

2. Make sure your nutrition profit center is simple and easy for your staff and you to operate, and is designed with the lowest overhead possible.

3. Build a nutrition profit center that provides recurring revenue month after month.

4. Make sure your nutrition profit center is designed to do what it does systematically and predictably every single time.

5. Work on building a totally integrated turnkey nutrition profit center that delivers exactly what you promise.

6. Brand your nutrition profit center to make it stand out from competitors.

Your practice's nutrition system holds the key to increasing your Income, your Profit, your Flow, and your Equity. Keep in mind that the money you make from selling nutrition depends not on how well your staff works, not on how well you work, but on how well your nutrition profit center works. A well-run practice with recurring revenues from a highly efficient ongoing Whole Body Alkaline Nutrition system is worth a lot of value to your practice and will produce a large amount of Equity.

Now that we've covered the all-important topic of money and how to make it work for your practice, let's see what Michael has to say about planning. ✤

CHAPTER 5

On the Subject of Planning

Michael E. Gerber

Luck is good planning, carefully executed.

—Anonymous

Another obvious oversight revealed in Steve and Peggy's story was the absence of true planning.

Every practitioner starting his or her own practice must have a plan. You should never begin to see patients without a plan in place. But, like Steve, most healthcare practitioners do exactly that.

A healthcare practitioner lacking a vision is simply someone who goes to work every day. Someone who is just doing it, doing it, doing it. Busy, busy, busy. Maybe making money, maybe not. Maybe getting something out of life, maybe not. Taking chances without really taking control.

The plan defines the objective and the process by which you will attain it. The plan encourages you to organize tasks into functions, and then helps people grasp the logic of each of those functions. This in turn permits you to bring new employees up to speed quickly.

There are numerous books and seminars on the subject of practice management, but they focus on making you a better healthcare practitioner. I want to teach you something else that you've never been taught before: how to be a manager. It has nothing to do with conventional practice management and everything to do with thinking like an entrepreneur.

The Planning Triangle

As we discussed in the Preface, every healthcare practice is a company, every healthcare business is a company, and every healthcare enterprise is a company. Yet the difference between the three is extraordinary. Although all three may offer healthcare services, how they do what they do is completely different.

The trouble with most companies owned by a practitioner is that they are dependent on the practitioner. That's because they're a practice—the smallest, most limited form a company can take. Practices are formed around the technician, whether healthcare practitioner or roofer.

You may choose in the beginning to form a practice, but you should understand its limitations. The company called a *practice* depends on the owner—that is, the healthcare practitioner who offers nutrition.

Consider the example of Sea Wellness & Nutrition Center. The patients don't come in asking for Dr. Douglas Sea, although he is one of the top wellness and nutrition practitioners around. After all, he can only handle so many cases a day and be in only one location at a time.

Yet he wants to offer his high-quality wellness and nutrition services to more people in the community. If he has reliable systems in place—systems that any qualified associate healthcare practitioner can learn to use—he has created a business and it can be replicated. Douglas can then go on to offer his wellness and nutrition services—which demand his guidance, not his presence—in a multitude of different settings.

He can open dozens of wellness and nutrition practices, none of which need Dr. Douglas Sea himself, except in the role of entrepreneur.

Is your company going to be a practice, a business, or an enterprise? Planning is crucial to answering this all-important question. Whatever you choose to do must be communicated by your plan, which is really three interrelated plans in one. We call it the Planning Triangle, and it looks like this:

- The Business Plan;
- The Practice; and
- The Completion Plan.

The three plans form a triangle, with the business plan at the base, the practice plan in the center, and the completion plan at the apex.

The business plan determines *who* you are (the business), the practice plan determines *what* you do (the specific focus of your practice), and the completion plan determines *how* you do it (the fulfillment process).

By looking at the Planning Triangle, we see that the three critical plans are interconnected. The connection between them is established by asking the following questions:

1. Who are we?
2. What do we do?
3. How do we do it?

Who are we? is purely a strategic question.
What do we do? is both a strategic and a tactical question.
How do we do it? is both a strategic and a tactical question.

Strategic questions shape the vision and destiny of your business, of which your practice is only one essential component. Tactical questions turn that vision into reality. Thus, strategic questions provide the foundation for tactical questions, just as the base provides the foundation for the middle and apex of your Planning Triangle.

First ask: What do we do, and how do we do it *strategically?*

And then: What do we do, and how do we do it *practically?*

Let's look at how the three plans will help you develop your practice.

The Business Plan

Your business plan will determine what you choose to do in your practice and the way you choose to do it. Without a business plan, your practice can do little more than survive. And even that will take more than a little luck.

Without a business plan, you're treading water in a deep pool with no shore in sight. You're working against the natural flow.

I'm not talking about the traditional business plan that is taught in business schools. No, this business plan reads like a story—the most important story you will ever tell.

Your business plan must clearly describe

- the business you are creating;
- the purpose it will serve;
- the vision it will pursue;
- the process through which you will turn that vision into a reality; and
- the way money will be used to realize your vision.

Build your business plan with *business* language, not *practice* language (the language of the healthcare practitioner). Make sure the plan focuses on matters of interest to your lenders and shareholders rather than just your technicians. It should rely on demographics and psychographics to tell you who buys and why; it should also include projections for return on investment and return on equity. Use it to detail both the market and the strategy through which you intend to become a leader in that market, not as a healthcare practitioner but as a business enterprise.

The business plan, though absolutely essential, is only one of three critical plans every healthcare practitioner needs to create and implement. Now let's take a look at the practice plan.

The Practice Plan

The practice plan includes everything a healthcare practitioner needs to know, have, and do in order to deliver his or her promise to a patient on time, every time.

Every task should prompt you to ask three questions:

1. What do I need to know?
2. What do I need to have?
3. What do I need to do?

What Do I Need to *Know?*

What information do I need to satisfy my promise on time, every time, exactly as promised? In order to recognize what you need to know, you must understand the expectations of others, including your patients, your associates, and other employees. Are you clear on those expectations? Don't make the mistake of assuming you know. Instead, create a need-to-know checklist to make sure you ask all the necessary questions.

A need-to-know checklist might look like this:

- What are the expectations of my patients?
- What are the expectations of my administrators?
- What are the expectations of my associate healthcare practitioners?
- What are the expectations of my staff?

What Do I Need to *Have*?

This question raises the issue of resources—namely, money, people, and time. If you don't have enough money to finance operations, how can you fulfill those expectations without creating cash-flow problems? If you don't have enough trained people, what happens then? And if you don't have enough time to manage your practice, what happens when you can't be in two places at once?

Don't assume that you can get what you need when you need it. Most often, you can't. And even if you can get what you need at the last minute, you'll pay dearly for it.

What Do I Need to *Do*?

The focus here is on actions to be started and finished. What do I need to do to fulfill the expectations of this patient on time, every time, exactly as promised? For example, what exactly are the steps to perform when offering nutrition as part of a patient's first visit protocol?

Your patients fall into distinct categories, and those categories make up your practice. The best healthcare practices will invariably focus on fewer and fewer categories as they discover the importance of doing one thing better than anyone else.

Answering the question *What do I need to do?* demands a series of action plans, including

- the objective to be achieved;
- the standards by which you will know that the objective has been achieved;
- the benchmarks you need to reach in order for the objective to be achieved;
- the function/person accountable for the completion of the benchmarks;
- the budget for the completion of each benchmark; and
- the time by which each benchmark must be completed.

Your action plans should become the foundation for the completion plan. And the reason you need completion plan is to ensure that everything you do is not only realistic but can also be managed.

The Completion Plan

If the practice plan gives you results and provides you with standards, the completion plan tells you everything you need to know about every benchmark in the practice plan—that is, how you're going to fulfill patient expectations on time, every time, as promised. In other words, how you're going to arrange a referral to another professional, set up an alkaline hydration station, conduct routine consultations, create nutritional wellness programs, or educate a patient on the importance of pH balancing.

The completion plan is essentially the operations manual, providing information about the details of doing tactical work. It is a guide to tell the people responsible for doing that work exactly how to do it.

Every completion plan becomes a part of the knowledge base of your business. No completion plan goes to waste. Every completion plan becomes a kind of textbook that explains to new employees or new associates joining your team how your practice operates in a way that distinguishes it from all other healthcare practices.

To return to an earlier example, the completion plan for making a Big Mac is explicitly described in the *McDonald's Operation Manual*, as is every completion plan needed to run a McDonald's business.

The completion plan for a healthcare practitioner offering nutrition might include the step-by-step details of how to nutritionally support acute and chronic inflammation starting on the patient's first visit-in contrast to how everyone else has learned to do it. Of course, every healthcare practitioner has been taught about inflammation and different ways to support it. Most doctors have learned to do it the same way every other doctor has learned to do it. But if you are going to stand out as unique in the minds of your patients, employees, and others, you must invent your own way of doing even ordinary things. Most of that value-added perception will come from your communication skills, your listening skills, your innovative skills in transforming an ordinary visit into a patient experience.

Perhaps you'll decide that a mandatory part of treating a patient with pre-diabetes is to chart out with words and pictures a comprehensive study and nutrition plan so the patient may gain a thorough knowledge of their condition. If no other healthcare practitioner your patient has seen has ever taken the time to explain the procedure, you'll immediately set yourself apart. You must constantly raise the questions: *How do we do it here? How should we do it here?*

The quality of your answers will determine how effectively you distinguish your practice from every other healthcare practitioner's practice.

Benchmarks

You can measure the movement of your practice—from what it is today to what it will be in the future—using business benchmarks. These are the goals you want your business to achieve during its lifetime.

Your benchmarks should include the following:

- Financial benchmarks
- Emotional benchmarks (the impact your practice will have on everyone who comes into contact with it)
- Performance benchmarks
- Patient benchmarks (Who are they? Why do they come to you? What does your practice give them that no one else does?)
- Employee benchmarks (How do you grow people? How do you find people who want to grow? How do you create a school in your practice that will teach your people skills they can't learn anywhere else?)

Your business benchmarks will reflect (1) the position your practice will hold in the minds and hearts of your patients, employees, and investors; and (2) how you intend to make that position a reality through the systems you develop.

Your benchmarks will describe how your management team will take shape and what systems you will need to develop so that your managers, just like McDonald's managers, will be able to produce the results for which they will be held accountable.

Benefits of the Planning Triangle

By implementing the Planning Triangle, you will discover:

- what your practice will look, act, and feel like when it's fully evolved;
- when that's going to happen;
- how much money you will make; and
- much, much more.

These, then, are the primary purposes of the three critical plans: (1) to clarify precisely what needs to be done to get what the health-care practitioner wants from his or her practice and life, and (2) to define the specific steps by which it will happen.

First *this* must happen, then *that* must happen. One, two, three. By monitoring your progress, step-by-step, you can determine whether you're on the right track.

That's what planning is all about. It's about creating a standard—a yardstick—against which you will be able to measure your performance.

Failing to create such a standard is like throwing a straw into a hurricane. Who knows where that straw will land?

Have you taken the leap? Have you accepted that the word *business* and the word *practice* are not synonymous? That a practice relies on the healthcare practitioner and a business relies on other people plus a system?

Because most healthcare practitioners are control freaks, 99 percent of today's doctors that offer nutrition are practices, not businesses.

The result, as a friend of mine says, is that "healthcare practitioners are spending all day stamping out fires when all around them the forest is ablaze. They're out of touch, and that doctor better take control of the practice before someone else does."

Because healthcare practitioners are never taught to think like businesspeople, the healthcare practitioner is forever at war with the businessperson. This is especially evident in large, multidiscipline practices, where bureaucrats (businesspeople) often try to control doctors (healthcare practitioners). They usually end up treating each other as combatants. In fact, the single greatest reason practitioners become entrepreneurs is to divorce such bureaucrats and to begin to reinvent the enterprise.

That's you. Now the divorce is over and a new love affair has begun. You're a healthcare practitioner with a plan! Who wouldn't want to do business with such a person?

Now let's take the next step in our strategic odyssey. Let's take a closer look at the subject of *management*. But before we do, let's see what Dr. Hayes has to say about planning. ✤

CHAPTER 6

Planning to Successfully Add Nutrition to Your Practice

Dr. Donald L. Hayes, DC

A goal without a plan is just a wish.

—Antoine de Saint-Exupery

Michael's last chapter provides you with a vivid road map on how to plan and create a thriving business. Of course, to pull that off and add a successful nutrition profit center to your existing specialty, you have to plan. And I'm here to tell you the plan that Michael outlined works.

Developing a plan can be difficult for healthcare practitioners. Due to the chaotic nature of running a practice, they never seem to have enough time to address the subject. Many who want to add nutrition simply go to a weekend post-graduate seminar, buy a bunch of vitamins, take them back to the office, and try to implement them, often with great difficulty. When you're as busy as we doctors are, who can take the time to plan? This common problem in healthcare must change and we've got to start now.

While I don't intend to repeat what Michael said in the last chapter, it's important for me to focus on a few key components of the planning process, as well as add some important distinctions specifically for you, the healthcare practitioner who wants to add nutrition to your practice.

The Planning Dilemma

You are a doctor who has always provided the highest quality healthcare to your patients and your community, but your practice has not grown into the profitable business you had hoped for, and now you feel frustrated. You figure that maybe if you could do something else, like add a successful nutrition profit center to the mix, it might turn things around. You barely have enough time now to work on your practice and you wonder how adding another clinical responsibility to your job duties is going to make things better.

Treating patients, doing examinations, conducting reports of findings, and filing good-old managed care paperwork are just a few of the things that prevent you from finding a time to conduct the strategic planning you need to do before adding nutrition to the office. And of course you need to stay current on your specialty by attending regular continuing education license renewal seminars, and maybe you really feel you should enroll in one of the major 300-plus-hour courses in nutrition before offering it to your patients. You are required to do all of this while also training staff and working with them to make sure they're doing the many small, vital things your patients need. You wonder if you'll ever be able to explain nutrition to your staff so they can handle the implementation process for you.

The Planning Process

This extensive list of responsibilities has forced a lot of doctors to view planning as a luxury reserved only for brand new practitioners, or those who have nothing but time on their hands. You, on the other hand, just got buzzed that all your treatment rooms are full, and because of the busy work of treating, treating, treating patients all day long, you'll have to postpone your plans to start selling your patients those vitamins you bought this past weekend.

The ironic truth is that by failing to plan, you are planning to fail. You must take the time to critically look at your practice as a business. You must create a plan on how to implement nutrition into your practice so you can use it to transform the practice into a business and on to a thriving enterprise.

I've learned that, regardless of all the busy work created by a practice, setting aside the time to plan must be a priority because it will help you make better business decisions in the future. The most important use of your time is committing your vision to paper and then detailing out the steps that make it a reality. This is not how doctors traditionally approach their practice, so if it feels uncomfortable to you, it must be right. You simply must set aside time for strategic planning.

The Purpose of Your Practice

The first E-Myth principle states that the purpose of your business is to serve you and your needs. Unfortunately, when most doctors get into private practice, this concept is replaced with the one where the healthcare practitioner's purpose seems to be solely to serve the practice.

That's why Michael's magical triangle (as I like to call it) from Chapter 5 is so important. For healthcare providers like you who want to successfully add a nutrition profit center to your practice, this is the tool that will set you free. All you need to do to gain that freedom and success is set aside a few days of quality time to map out how nutrition will fit into your practice. Asking the three key questions is the best starting point: *Who are we? What do we do? How do we do it?*

It's more than likely that you never asked these questions when you started your business. But now, as you add nutrition into your practice, you're going to be different. So let's start the planning process and design these plans to work in your practice.

Your Nutrition Business Plan – Who You Are

Your plan should not be something you think your banker is going to read, it must be a story about why you feel adding nutrition to your practice is so important. You're doing this for a much bigger reason than simply to make more money. It has a purpose in your community that will affect a lot of people like staff, suppliers, and, of course, your patients. Your nutrition business plan is your vision for how you're going to pull the whole thing off.

To get started on your plan, it may be helpful to either book some time away from the office or shut down one of your least busy work-days. This way, you can spend some quality time digging deep into your purpose for adding nutrition and detailing exactly how it fits into your original intentions. One of your first exercises should be to honestly look at the field of nutrition and decide exactly what you want to accomplish. This will keep you focused and ensure that you don't wander down a path that diverges from your core objectives.

Regardless how anxious you may be to add nutrition, if you approach it without your bigger purpose in mind, your plan will fail, regardless of how much money you generate. Pull out all the stops and create the nutrition profit center that you want. And who knows, you may find yourself re-energized about designing this component of your practice all over again.

This process is not easy. It may take some real searching to come face-to-face with the challenges of adding nutrition, but please don't rob yourself of this opportunity or dismiss it as being unimportant. To be happy in your line of work, you need to align yourself with a higher purpose—a solid reason for providing nutrition to each and every one of your patients.

The fact is, this is your life. It's the way you support yourself and your family. Your practice is where most of your time will be spent, so you better enjoy using nutrition as part of the practice as much as you enjoy providing your primary services. If you don't have passion for offering nutrition in your practice, you're running the risk of failing, because you'll be competing against other doctors who truly believe in the benefits of adding nutrition to their specialty.

Once the intention to add nutrition to your practice has been settled on, you'll begin to feel the impact in many different ways. Your practice as a whole will actually become easier, as nutrition that was only recently non-existent will suddenly seem to fit. The greatest benefit of this process is that it will help you avoid all distractions that come across your desk from the field of nutrition that don't serve the direction you've chosen. As you begin to offer nutrition in your practice, the word will get out and you'll have every major nutritional manufacturer chasing you down to carry their product line. Some of the products may sound superior, and some will promise more money and better health for your patient, but if they are not congruent with your bigger purpose, then you need to just say no.

This is a very difficult thing to do; you need to have complete confidence in your nutrition profit center so you can turn away everything else that isn't part of your specific nutrition business plan. Even though many of the other nutrition opportunities will seem to be good at the time, typically they will do nothing but distract you from your plan, waste your energy, and scatter your focus. I have found that those who truly succeed with nutrition in a big way succeed because they create a practice they love, choose an appropriate course, and stay on it.

When you are able to stay on your chosen path, you're reinforcing your commitment to follow your goals. This kind of dedication gives you the confidence to build the nutrition business you want. Not allowing yourself to get distracted and saying no to every incompatible nutrition opportunity that comes along sends a message to your staff and your patients that you're serious about your nutrition business plan and devoted to the goals you set in motion.

Remember how important that is! The best person to decide what nutritional approach is best for your practice is you! Pick your direction and then stay the course – your unwavering commitment will inspire everyone within your practice.

Your Nutrition Practice Plan – What You Do

The next step in the planning process is creating a snapshot of your nutrition profit center—what Michael calls the "what we do" piece of the puzzle. This includes the income you expect to generate using nutrition, the specific nutrition products you will offer, and, of course, the amount of time you'll need to accomplish your predetermined goals. Add to that the way the product will be positioned in your office, the initial number of staff you will need, and projections of future growth, and you begin to see your nutrition practice plan come to life.

By looking forward and projecting how your nutrition profit center will grow, you can take full advantage of your plan. Project what additional services patients will need or want so much that they'll reach in their pockets and pay to have them. If you ask your patients the right questions, you'll be impressed by their thoughtful responses and invaluable feedback.

The outcome of offering nutrition as an integral part of your practice, in concert with what patients want (typically relief from their main complaint as soon as possible) is completely different from what most doctors expect. The days of putting a few "me-too" nutrition products at the front desk and thinking patients will buy them is over, and it never worked anyway. Today, having a nutrition marketing system in place is a powerful way to attract new patients who have an eye on nutrition before you ever see them. This is the most compelling way for you to become the voice and vision of nutritional wellness awareness.

Of course, the marketing arena is always changing, but one thing is timeless: patients stay connected and repurchase their nutrition from the doctor who stays connected to them. You should consider using an effective marketing strategy in your nutrition profit center to maintain a lifelong relationship with your patients.

Your Nutrition Completion Plan – How You Do It

Without a doubt, your nutrition business development process will revolve around establishing and documenting systems for each part of your nutrition practice. This part of the plan, more than any other, will immediately turn an inefficient and disorganized practice that offers nutrition into a successful nutrition business that will run itself.

There should be a system in place for every nutrition job, function, and duty that is conducted in the practice on even a semi-regular basis. You must have a system for developing nutrition leads and a system for converting those leads into new patients. You need a system for presenting the nutrition products in the office, a system for explaining the nutrition, and a system for answering nutrition-related questions. You'll also need a system for ordering, receiving, and stocking the products, and a system outlining how patients pay for the products. You'll need a system for hiring new staff, for training them on the nutrition products, for giving them performance reviews, and for letting a staff member go when their performance is not meeting the expected nutrition practice goals.

Do you get the big idea here?

You need a complete set of systems that detail every area of your nutrition practice. When new staff members come on board, they should be able to review the nutrition operating manual for your practice, which not only outlines your nutrition policies and goals, but also documents the proper way to perform their job as well as the way their performance will be measured. Until these kinds of systems are firmly in place in the practice, you are still just a practice that sells a few bottles of vitamins, as opposed to a full-fledged nutrition business.

Doctors often ask me why all these systems are so vital to something as simple as nutrition. Any staff person can hold up a bottle of vitamins and offer them to patients, right? That may be true, but it doesn't mean they understand the specifics of your unique nutrition system.

Your nutrition completion plan will have everyone singing the same song. It ensures that each and every one of your patients is offered Whole Body Alkaline Nutrition to support their healthy inflammatory response in a consistent way. It guarantees that every patient has the opportunity to accept or decline the use of nutrition for their natural relief efforts.

Your completion plan allows your nutrition profit center to evolve by questioning "the way you've always done nutrition" and then looking for "the way you should be doing nutrition" instead. When you set up these types of nutrition protocols, everyone in the practice will get on board. Now, instead of having individual "people issues" when it comes to problems with nutrition, you have system issues which you and your staff can resolve together. This creates a major shift in the way you practice nutrition.

You, your associates, and your staff will feel more confident about the way you do your jobs and your patients will reap the rewards of your efficiency. Your plan will identify the nutrition profit center goals you want to accomplish, outline the steps required to do it, and establish a system for tracking those steps and monitoring performance. There is no easier way to manage your nutrition business than this.

When you implement these systems, you'll find that it's much easier to position your practice as a leader in the marketplace. And now it seems the perfect time to move on from planning and take a look at what Michael has to say about the inner workings of your team; primarily, that of management. ❧

On the Subject of Management

Michael E. Gerber

"Management" means, in the last analysis, the substitution of thought for brawn and muscle, of knowledge for folklore and superstition, and of cooperation for force.

—Peter F. Drucker, *People and Performance*

Every healthcare practitioner, including Steve, eventually faces the issues of management. Most face it badly.

Why do so many healthcare practitioners suffer from a kind of paralysis when it comes to dealing with management? Why are so few able to get their practice to work the way they want it to and to run it on time? Why are their managers (if they have any) seemingly so inept?

There are two main problems. First, the healthcare practitioner usually abdicates accountability for management by hiring an office manager. Thus, the healthcare practitioner is working hand in glove with someone who is supposed to do the managing. But the healthcare practitioner is unmanageable himself!

The healthcare practitioner doesn't think like a manager because he doesn't think he is a manager. He's a practitioner! He rules the roost. And so he gets the office manager to take care of stuff like scheduling appointments, keeping his calendar, collecting receivables, hiring/firing, and much more.

Second, no matter who does the managing, they usually have a completely dysfunctional idea of what it means to manage. They're trying to manage people, contrary to what is needed.

We often hear that a good manager must be a "people person." Someone who loves to nourish, figure out, support, care for, teach, baby, monitor, mentor, direct, track, motivate, and, if all else fails, threaten or beat up her people.

Don't believe it. Management has far less to do with people than you've been led to believe.

In fact, despite the claims of every management book written by management gurus (who have seldom managed anything), no one—with the exception of a few bloodthirsty tyrants—has ever learned how to manage people.

And the reason is simple: *People are almost impossible to manage.*

Yes, it's true. People are unmanageable. They're inconsistent, unpredictable, unchangeable, unrepentant, irrepressible, and generally impossible.

Doesn't knowing this make you feel better? Now you understand why you've had all those problems! Do you feel the relief, the heavy stone lifted from your chest?

The time has come to fully understand what management is really all about. Rather than managing *people*, management is really all about managing a *process*, a step-by-step way of doing things, which, combined with other processes, becomes a system. For example:

- The process for on-time scheduling
- The process for answering the telephone
- The process for greeting a patient
- The process for organizing patient files
- The process for integrating nutritional supplements

Thus, a process is the step-by-step way of doing something over time. Considered as a whole, these processes are a system:

- The on-time scheduling system
- The telephone answering system
- The patient greeting system
- The file organization system
- The nutritional operating system

Instead of managing people, then, the truly effective manager has been taught a system for managing a process through which people get things done.

More precisely, managers and their people, *together*, manage the processes—the systems—that comprise your business. Management is less about *who* gets things done in your business than about *how* things get done.

In fact, great managers are not fascinated with people, but with how things get done through people. Great managers are masters at figuring out how to get things done effectively and efficiently through people using extraordinary systems.

Great managers constantly ask key questions, such as:

- What is the result we intend to produce?
- Are we producing that result every single time?
- If we're not producing that result every single time, why not?
- If we are producing that result every single time, how could we produce even better results?
- Do we lack a system? If so, what would that system look like if we were to create it?
- If we have a system, why aren't we using it?

And so forth.

In short, a great manager can leave the office fully assured that it will run at least as well as it does when he or she is physically in the room.

Great managers are those who use a great management system. A system that shouts, "This is *how* we manage here." Not "This is *who* manages here."

In a truly effective company, how you manage is always more important than who manages. Provided a system is in place, how you manage is transferable, whereas who manages isn't. *How* you manage can be taught, whereas *who* manages can't be.

When a company is dependent on *who* manages—Katie, Kim, or Kevin—that business is in serious jeopardy. Because when Katie, Kim, or Kevin leaves, that business has to start over again. What an enormous waste of time and resources!

Even worse, when a company is dependent on *who* manages, you can bet all the managers in that business are doing their own thing. What could be more unproductive than ten managers who each manage in a unique way? How in the world could you possibly manage those managers?

The answer is: You can't. Because it takes you right back to trying to manage *people* again.

And, as I hope you now know, that's impossible.

In this chapter, I often refer to managers in the plural. I know that most healthcare practitioners only have one manager—the office manager. And so you may be thinking that a management system isn't so important in a small healthcare practice. After all, the office manager does whatever an office manager does (and thank God, because you don't want to do it).

But if your practice is ever going to turn into the business it could become, and if that business is ever going to turn into the enterprise of your dreams, then the questions you ask about how the office manager manages your affairs are critical ones. Because until you come to grips with your dual role as owner and key employee, and the relationship your manager has to those two roles, your practice/business/enterprise will never realize its potential. Thus the need for a management system.

Management System

What, then, is a management system?

The E-Myth says that a management system is the method by which every manager innovates, quantifies, orchestrates, and then monitors the systems through which your practice produces the results you expect.

According to the E-Myth, a manager's job is simple:

A manager's job is to invent the systems through which the owner's vision is consistently and faithfully manifested at the operating level of the business.

Which brings us right back to the purpose of your business and the need for an entrepreneurial vision.

Are you beginning to see what I'm trying to share with you? That your business is one single thing? And that all the subjects we're discussing here—money, planning, management, and so on—are all about doing one thing well?

That one thing is the one thing your practice is intended to do: distinguish your business from all others.

It is the manager's role to make certain it all fits. And it's your role as entrepreneur to make sure your manager knows what the business is supposed to look, act, and feel like when it's finally done. As clearly as you know how, you must convey to your manager what you know to be true—your vision, your picture of the business when it's finally done. In this way, your vision is translated into your manager's marching orders every day he or she reports to work.

Unless that vision is embraced by your manager, you and your people will suffer from the tyranny of routine. And your business will suffer from it, too.

Now let's move on to *people*. Because, as we know, it's people who are causing all our problems. But before we do, let's see what Dr. Hayes has to say about management. ❧

Making Nutrition Manageable

Dr. Donald L. Hayes, DC

Good management is the art of making problems so interesting and their solutions so constructive that everyone wants to get to work and deal with them.

—Paul Hawken

I f you want to offer a nutritional solution for many of the common health challenges your patients face, it's very important to make the process manageable.

Most healthcare practitioners find it very difficult to manage nutrition inside a busy practice. During my many years of consulting, I would urge doctors to closely examine their nutrition profits. A few doctors would find that they were earning a small profit, and some others would realize that they were losing money, while the majority would discover that they were just breaking even. Most were shocked by the sobering news that they were breaking even or losing money, and nearly all would immediately rationalize it away by saying something like, "Well, we're not offering nutrition to make money anyway."

I think this answer made them feel less embarrassed about their poor performance. There's no need to be embarrassed upon learning you're a poor manager, it just means that you need a better management system.

Nutrition is a multi-billion dollar cash industry. In the hands of a healthcare practitioner using a good management system, making profit is not difficult. If doctors are offering nutrition for the right reasons, in tandem with a proven management system, there is absolutely no reason that it won't be extremely profitable.

Doctors Don't Sell Nutrition, Systems Do

The fact that most doctors have difficulty selling nutrition in their practices doesn't concern most nutrition manufacturers—but it should!

When doctors offer nutrition without a system, they lose money, and it's not long before many of them quit trying to sell it altogether. I've lost count of the number of doctors who have told me they quit selling nutrition because they were losing money. Most of them said they liked the idea of offering it, but since it didn't make financial sense, they stopped. A doctor's decision to stop offering nutrition has many consequences: it is a major loss for patients who are deprived of the opportunity to utilize a natural supplement in conjunction with their care plan, and it drives nutrition sales into retail vitamin stores. Market research clearly shows that patients who go to alternative healthcare practitioners want to buy nutrition supplements, so if their doctor doesn't offer them, they'll buy them somewhere else.

Doctors are Poor Managers

Business education and people management skills are not part of any healthcare curriculum I've ever seen. So it's no surprise that most healthcare practitioners don't know how to manage a business—they simply haven't had the training.

The good news for doctors is what Michael made so clear in the last chapter: "People do not manage; systems that people follow do." So the primary reason healthcare practitioners are unsuccessful at offering nutrition is because they don't set up nutrition systems that their staff can easily follow.

Doctors often shift the responsibility of selling nutrition away from themselves and on to an office manager or a staff person. This leaves the doctor free from any accountability and frankly, it's bad management. When you design a system for something as important as using nutrition to help improve a patient's outcome, the responsibility for this system should rest squarely on your shoulders. I don't know why so many doctors avoid this key responsibility. If you want to offer nutrition, you must set up a system that will be followed to the letter because if you don't, your nutrition products just won't get sold!

Designing a Nutrition Management System

You've decided to offer nutrition because you feel it's the best thing for your patient's health. So you might as well do it right. And in order to do it right, you have to keep in mind what Michael says: "management" means managing a process, a step-by-step method of offering nutrition which, combined with the other functions of the practice, ultimately becomes an efficient nutrition system.

To begin, focus on creating nutrition systems that your staff can follow to manage the practice's day-to-day nutritional tasks. In other words, you and your staff together will manage the daily nutrition operations, which make up the nutrition systems that comprise the nutrition business. Remember, it's not about who does what, it's all about how things get done!

When you take the time to develop a nutrition system that outlines exactly how procedures must be followed every day, you can rest assured that the system will be consistently efficient day-to-day without any supervision on your part.

This is critical, because you do not have the time to constantly oversee routine nutritional procedures. If your practice ever becomes dependent on one nutrition staff person—the only one who knows the product line or the only one who can sell the products to patients—you will be sitting in a very precarious position that could expose you to huge financial loss. When the nutrition system is in place, it can be operated by any and all staff members, leaving you free to focus on your patients' care without any distractions.

Remember, Michael has helped thousands of business owners establish management systems, regardless of the type of business they operate. Nutrition management is no different, it's simply a method by which the healthcare practitioner innovates, quantifies, orchestrates, and then monitors the nutrition systems that allow the practice to flourish.

If you want to offer nutrition, your job is very clear: simply develop nutrition systems that support your practice vision. This further demonstrates the importance of establishing both the purpose of your nutrition profit center and your entrepreneurial vision.

It all boils down to one, key thing: making sure your nutrition profit center stands out head and shoulders above every other practice that offers nutrition. It's your role as the healthcare practitioner to make sure that all associates and staff members know why you offer nutrition and how it makes a difference in the lives of your patients. Your staff must know that your practice vision includes the use of nutrition not just for some patients, but for all patients.

When you are successful at getting your staff to embrace your vision, your nutrition profit center will prosper and your patients will thrive. Now that you know and understand this important principle, it's time to learn what Michael has to say about dealing with people in your practice. ✤

On the Subject of People

Michael E. Gerber

We are not human beings having a spiritual experience. We are spiritual beings having a human experience.

—Teilhard de Chardin

Every healthcare practitioner I've ever met has complained about people.

About employees: "They come in late, they go home early, they have the focus of an antique camera!"

About insurance companies: "They're living in a non-parallel universe!"

About patients: "They want me to repair thirty years of bad habits and inadequate care!"

People, people, people. Every healthcare practitioner's nemesis. And at the heart of it all are the people who work for you.

"By the time I tell them how to do it, I could have done it twenty times myself!" "How come nobody listens to what I say?"

"Why is it nobody ever does what I ask them to do?" Does this sound like you?

So what's the problem with people? To answer that, think back to the last time you walked into a healthcare practitioner's office. What did you see in the people's faces?

Most people working in healthcare are harried. You can see it in their expressions. They're negative. They're bad-spirited. They're humorless. And with good reason. After all, they're surrounded by people who have headaches, chronic pain or—worst-case scenario—a serious disease. Patients are looking for nurturing, for empathy, for care. And many are either terrified or depressed. They don't want to be there.

Is it any wonder employees at most practices are disgruntled? They're surrounded by unhappy people all day. They're answering the same questions 24/7. And most of the time, the healthcare practitioner has no time for them. He or she is too busy leading a dysfunctional life.

Working with people brings great joy—and monumental frustration. And so it is with healthcare practitioners and their people. But why? And what can we do about it?

Let's look at the typical healthcare practitioner—who this person is and isn't.

Most healthcare practitioners are unprepared to use other people to get results. Not because they can't find people, but because they are fixated on getting the results themselves. In other words, most healthcare practitioners are not the businesspeople they need to be, but *technicians suffering from an entrepreneurial seizure.*

Am I talking about you? What were you doing before you became an entrepreneur?

Were you an associate healthcare practitioner working for a large multiclinic organization? A midsized practice? A small practice?

Didn't you imagine owning your own practice as the way out?

Didn't you think that because you knew how to do the technical work—because you knew so much about injuries, health conditions, and wellness—that you were automatically prepared to create a practice that does that type of work?

Didn't you figure that by creating your own practice, you could dump the boss once and for all? How else to get rid of that impossible person, the one driving you crazy, the one who never let you do your own thing, the one who was the main reason you decided to take the leap into a business of your own in the first place?

Didn't you start your own practice so that you could become your own boss?

And didn't you imagine that once you became your own boss, you would be free to do whatever you wanted to do—and to take home *all* the money?

Honestly, isn't that what you imagined? So you went into business for yourself and immediately dived into work.

Doing it, doing it, doing it.

Busy, busy, busy.

Until one day you realized (or maybe not) that you were doing all of the work. You were doing everything you knew how to do, plus a lot more you knew nothing about. Building sweat equity, you thought.

In reality, a technician suffering from an entrepreneurial seizure.

You were just hoping to make a buck in your own practice. And sometimes you did earn a wage. But other times you didn't. You were the one signing the checks, all right, but they went to other people.

Does this sound familiar? Is it driving you crazy?

Well, relax, because we're going to show you the right way to do it this time.

Read carefully. Be mindful of the moment. You are about to learn the secret you've been waiting for all your working life.

The People Law

It's critical to know this about the working life of healthcare practitioners who own their own practice: *Without people, you don't own a practice, you own a job.* And it can be the worst job in the world because you're working for a lunatic! (Nothing personal—but we've got to face facts.)

Let me state what every healthcare practitioner knows: Without people, you're going to have to do it all yourself. Without human help, you're doomed to try to do too much. This isn't a breakthrough idea, but it's amazing how many healthcare practitioners ignore the truth. They end up knocking themselves out, ten to twelve hours a day. They try to do more, but less actually gets done.

The load can double you over and leave you panting. In addition to the work you're used to doing, you may also have to do the books. And the organizing. And the filing. You'll have to do the planning and the scheduling. When you own your own practice, the daily minutiae are never-ceasing—as I'm sure you've found out. Like painting the Golden Gate Bridge, it's endless. Which puts it beyond the realm of human possibility. Until you discover how to get it done by somebody else, it will continue on and on until you're a burned-out husk.

But with others helping you, things will start to drastically improve. If, that is, you truly understand how to engage people in the work you need them to do. When you learn how to do that, when you learn how to replace yourself with other people—people trained in your system—then your practice can really begin to grow. Only then will you begin to experience true freedom yourself.

What typically happens is that healthcare practitioners, knowing they need help answering the phone, filing, and so on, go out and find people who can do these things. Once they delegate these duties, however, they rarely spend any time with the employee. Deep down they feel it's not important *how* these things get done; it's only important that they get done.

They fail to grasp the requirement for a system that makes people their greatest asset rather than their greatest liability. A system so reliable that if Chris dropped dead tomorrow, Leslie could do exactly what Chris did. That's where the People Law comes in.

The People Law says that each time you add a new person to your practice using an intelligent (turnkey) system that works, you expand your reach. And you can expand your reach almost infinitely! People allow you to be everywhere you want to be simultaneously, without actually having to be there in the flesh.

People are to a healthcare practitioner what a record was to Frank Sinatra. A Sinatra record could be (and still is) played in a million places at the same time, regardless of where Frank was. And every record sale produced royalties for Sinatra (or his estate).

With the help of other people, Sinatra created a quality recording that faithfully replicated his unique talents, then made sure it was marketed and distributed, and the revenue managed.

Your people can do the same thing for you. All *you* need to do is to create a "recording"—a system—of your unique talents, your special way of practicing healthcare, and then replicate it, market it, distribute it, and manage the revenue.

Isn't that what successful businesspeople do? Make a "recording" of their most effective ways of doing business? In this way, they provide a turnkey solution to their patients' problems. A system solution that really works.

Doesn't your practice offer the same potential for you that records did for Sinatra (and now for his heirs)? The ability to produce income without having to go to work every day?

Isn't that what your people could be for you? The means by which your system for practicing healthcare could be faithfully replicated?

But first you've got to have a system. You have to create a unique way of doing business that you can teach to your people, that you can manage faithfully, and that you can replicate consistently, just like McDonald's.

Because without such a system, without such a "recording," without a unique way of doing business that really works, all you're left with is people doing their own thing. And that is almost always a recipe for chaos. Rather than guaranteeing consistency, it encourages mistake after mistake after mistake.

And isn't that how the problem started in the first place? People doing whatever *they* perceived they needed to do, regardless of what you wanted? People left to their own devices, with no regard for the costs of their behavior? The costs to you?

In other words, people without a system.

Can you imagine what would have happened to Frank Sinatra if he had followed that example? If every one of his recordings had been done differently? Imagine a million different versions of "My Way." It's unthinkable.

Would you buy a record like that? What if Frank were having a bad day? What if he had a sore throat?

Please hear this: The People Law is unforgiving. Without a systematic way of doing business, people are more often a liability than an asset. Unless you prepare, you'll find out too late which ones are which.

The People Law says that without a specific system for doing business; without a specific system for recruiting, hiring, and training your people to use that system; and without a specific system for managing and improving your systems, your practice will always be a crapshoot.

Do you want to roll the dice with your practice at stake? Unfortunately, that is what most healthcare practitioners are doing.

The People Law also says that you can't effectively delegate your responsibilities unless you have something specific to delegate. And that something specific is a way of doing business that works!

Frank Sinatra is gone, but his voice lives on. And someone is still counting his royalties. That's because Sinatra had a system that worked.

Do you? Let's see if Dr. Hayes does, and then we will move on to the subject of associate practitioners. ❖

People Make Nutrition Successful

Dr. Donald L. Hayes, DC

The good leader is he who the people revere. The great leader is he who the people say, "We did it ourselves."

—Lao Tzu

O nce you've decided to put a nutrition system in place that compliments and supports your healthcare specialty, you now need to turn your attention to what will be the foundation of your nutrition success, your people.

How Most Nutrition Profit Centers Start

Here's a typical scenario that might be familiar to you: A newly-minted healthcare practitioner—we'll call him Dr. Marty—attends some type of post-graduate training or license renewal seminar where he hears about some exciting new research that validates the use of a particular supplement for conditions he frequently sees in his practice. Dr. Marty gets very excited because he wants to do the most good for his patients, so he purchases a bunch of the product and hopes to use it to help his patients get well faster.

Dr. Marty is not really considering how he will implement it. But he remembers his nutrition training from school and he figures it won't be that difficult to sell this product to his patients.

Every chiropractor, for instance, regardless of where they obtained their professional education, receives between 300 and 400 hours of graduate-level nutrition training. Many other chiropractors go on to acquire hundreds of additional hours in nutrition and post-graduate degrees in the field, but none of them ever get any training on how to promote nutrition in their practice.

In other words, none of them have the foggiest idea of what a nutrition system is or how to create one, let alone how to implement it into a busy practice.

So what really happens to Dr. Marty is usually one of two things. Here's the first way it might happen: Dr. Marty takes the product back to his office and gives it to a staff person, who has even less training on the use of nutrition than he does. He delegates all responsibility to them, making them the official office nutritionist. This is a quick and easy recipe for disaster, because the staff person just throws the products up on a shelf at the front desk where they typically sit for about two years until they expire, and Dr. Marty's spouse, while cleaning the office one day, decides to toss the expired products in the trash.

Here's the other way it might play out: Dr. Marty arrives back at the office after the seminar and begins telling a few patients about the products. He tries to remember the science and the research that supports this supplement. He attempts to recall all the health benefits of the product, everything he was taught over the weekend. It's hard to remember all the particulars, and he finds it difficult to explain his purchase to his staff and his patients. With a great deal of uncertainty, as soon as Dr. Marty encounters some resistance from his patients, he stops recommending the products. He worries that his patients are starting to feel like he's too pushy or that they are starting to think of him as a "vitamin salesman."

In the midst of his busy schedule, Dr. Marty starts to forget why he bought the product in the first place. Once again, the product finds its way onto that shelf at the front desk where it awaits its inevitable fate of expiration and cleaning day disposal.

Obviously, this is not a model for success with nutrition, it's a model for total failure. Have you experienced Dr. Marty's predicament? If not, I'd bet you know someone who has.

If either of these outcomes has done some damage to your practice in the past, or if you're worried about becoming just another precautionary tale, I'm here to reassure you that offering nutrition in your practice doesn't have to end as badly as it did for Dr. Marty.

Let's look more closely at why Dr. Marty's situation is so common and learn how to prevent it from happening to you. The secret to unlocking the world of nutrition is about to appear.

An Operating System Makes Offering Nutrition Easy

Dr. Marty wasn't lacking in technical training, but he failed because he couldn't easily articulate his knowledge to his people. If you combine your knowledge of nutrition with a simple operating system, and then teach that system to your people so they can follow it easily, you can avoid Dr. Marty's fate.

In my nutrition boot camps, I would teach all the science and research on nutrition that doctors love so much, but I would also make sure to teach a nutrition operating system that they could follow once they got back to their office and the reality of a busy private practice set in.

In the nutrition company I currently own, I offer free strategic tools and staff training to every one of our healthcare practitioner clients to help them create their nutrition system. I feel it's my responsibility to help you "get out of your own way" and better utilize your people so your practice can be successful and you can expand the reach of your mission to help patients resolve health challenges and live better.

In order to achieve these goals, you have to remember something that Dr. Marty forgot—the People Law.

The People Law Applied to Nutrition

In the last chapter, Michael told us all about the People Law and how unforgiving it is. The bottom line is that if you offer nutrition without a system (like Dr. Marty did), your staff will become a liability instead of an asset.

I agree with Michael that most doctors complain constantly about people, both staff and patients. One of the main reasons for this is that doctors know almost nothing about how to effectively delegate. If you want your nutrition profit center to be successful, you've got to learn this crucial skill. Without staff members who are trained to follow a nutrition system, you will be stuck doing all the work yourself and it just won't get done!

And yet, as we learned from Dr. Marty, nutrition is one of those businesses that you can't effectively delegate away as the owner/ doctor unless you have specific system guidelines in place. You can't just hand all the nutrition work over to your staff without detailed instructions. If you do that, you might as well throw your nutrition products in the trash yourself.

The People Law of Nutrition says that a specific system for recruiting, hiring, and training your people on how to use nutrition in your office is absolutely vital to the growth of your nutrition profits. If you don't support your people, you won't have a business at all.

So let's revisit our good friend Dr. Marty and see how he's faring now that he's properly applied the People Law to his practice.

Excited as he is to get started with the nutrition products he purchased at the seminar over the weekend, Dr. Marty hears Michael's voice in his head and realizes that he'll need a specific system in place before he can hand over every detail of his nutrition profit center to his staff. Rather than impulsively throwing the products up on a shelf, Dr. Marty closely examines the marketing and management tools that came with the nutrition products he bought, and then takes some time every night that very week to develop a nutrition profit center system that is in alignment with his existing mission.

Next, he makes sure to specifically outline every nutrition procedure in a clear and concise way so that every associate and staff member knows exactly how to operate the system. It isn't long before all of his people are engaged and the system is humming along— Dr. Marty has essentially replaced himself with his people who are trained in his system.

Imagine Dr. Marty's happy outcome as your own: now that your system is running smoothly, you have the freedom to get back to your passion and stay focused entirely on your patients, knowing all the while that they are getting the nutritional support they need. Because of your system, you can start growing your business into the enterprise that you have always envisioned. And once your enterprise expands, you may find you need to take on associates to handle the patient load. Before you do so, let's find out more about Michael's thoughts on associates. ✤

On the Subject of Associates

Michael E. Gerber

*Associate yourself with men of good quality if you esteem your own
reputation, for 'tis better to be alone than in bad company.*

—George Washington

I f you are a sole practitioner—that is you're selling only yourself—
then your company called a practice will never make the leap
to a company called a business. The progression from practice
to business to enterprise demands that you hire other healthcare
practitioners to do what you do (or don't do). Contractors call
these people subcontractors; for our purposes, we'll refer to them as
associate healthcare practitioners.

Long ago, God said, "Let there be healthcare practitioners. And
so they never forget who they are in my creation, let them be damned
forever to hire people exactly like themselves." Enter the associates.

Merriam-Webster's Collegiate Dictionary, Eleventh Edition, defines
sub as "under, below, secretly; inferior to." If associate healthcare

practitioner are like sub-practitioners, you could define an associate as "an inferior individual contracted to perform part or all of another's contract."

In other words, you, the healthcare practitioner, make a conscious decision to hire someone "inferior" to you to fulfill *your* commitment to *your* patient, for which you are ultimately and solely liable.

Why in the world do we do these things to ourselves? Where will this madness lead? It seems the blind are leading the blind, and the blind are paying others to do it. And when a healthcare practitioner is blind, you *know* there's a problem!

It's time to step out of the darkness and come into the light. Forget about being Mr. Nice Guy—it's time to do things that work.

Solving the Associate Healthcare Practitioner Problem

Let's say you're about to hire an associate healthcare practitioner. Someone who has specific skills: technique, rehab, whatever. It all starts with choosing the right personnel. After all, these are people to whom you are delegating your responsibility and for whose behavior you are completely liable. Do you really want to leave that choice to chance? Are you that much of a gambler? I doubt it.

If you've never worked with your new associate, how do you really know he or she is skilled? For that matter, what does "skilled" mean?

For you to make an intelligent decision about this associate healthcare practitioner, you must have a working definition of the word *skilled*. Your challenge is to know *exactly* what your expectations are, then to make sure your other healthcare practitioners operate with precisely the same expectations. Failure here almost assures a breakdown in your relationship.

I want you to write the following on a piece of paper: "By *skilled*, I mean . . . " Once you create your personal definition, it will become a standard for you and your practice, for your patients, and for your associate healthcare practitioners.

A standard, according to *Webster's Eleventh*, is something "set up and established by authority as a rule for the measure of quantity, weight, extent, value, or quality."

Thus, your goal is to establish a measure of quality control, a standard of skill, which you will apply to all your associate health-care practitioners. More important, you are also setting a standard for the performance of your company.

By creating standards for your selection of other healthcare practitioners—standards of skill, performance, integrity, financial stability, and experience—you have begun the powerful process of building a practice that can operate exactly as you expect it to.

By carefully thinking about exactly what to expect, you have already begun to improve your practice.

In this enlightened state, you will see the selection of your associates as an opportunity to define what you (1) intend to provide for your patients, (2) expect from your employees, and (3) demand for your life.

Powerful stuff, isn't it? Are you up to it? Are you ready to feel your rising power?

Don't rest on your laurels just yet. Defining those standards is only the first step you need to take. The second step is to create an *associate healthcare practitioner development system.*

An associate healthcare practitioner development system is an action plan designed to tell you what you are looking for in an associate. It includes the exact benchmarks, accountabilities, timing of fulfillment, and budget you will assign to the process of looking for associate healthcare practitioners, identifying them, recruiting them, interviewing them, training them, managing their work, auditing their performance, compensating them, reviewing them regularly, and terminating or rewarding them for their performance.

All of these things must be documented—actually *written down*—if they're going to make any difference to you, your associate healthcare practitioners, your managers, or your bank account!

And then you've got to persist with that system, come hell or high water. Just as Ray Kroc did. Just as Walt Disney did. Just as Sam Walton did.

This leads us to our next topic of discussion: the subject of *estimating*. But first, let's see what Dr. Hayes has to say on the subject of associate healthcare practitioners. ✤

CHAPTER 12

Associates Are Good Business

Dr. Donald L. Hayes, DC

It's better to hang out with people better than you. Pick out associates whose behavior is better than yours and you'll drift in that direction.
—Warren Buffett

Running a successful nutrition profit center and building a successful nutrition business are two totally different things. You own your nutrition profit center, but if you want to grow that practice into a nutrition business and eventually establish a nutrition enterprise that adds Equity to your practice, you will need to consider hiring and training associates.

Twenty years ago it was commonplace for nearly all graduating chiropractors to become associates in successful practices, and I took that approach myself. Most associate relationships proceed in one of two ways: either the associate leaves after an agreed upon amount of time (typically a year) to open a new practice, or the associate agrees to purchase the healthcare practitioner's existing practice.

Today, due to the changes in insurance reimbursement and managed care, most healthcare practitioners who own successful practices don't feel they can afford to hire associates. This creates a problem for both the healthcare practitioners in practice and the new healthcare practitioners coming out of school.

The established healthcare practitioners no longer have access to newly licensed practitioners who are willing to work for a year in their practice. They lose the opportunity to have someone assist them by sharing the patient treatment duties, performing examinations, and doing nutrition consultations, all of which allow the healthcare practitioners to take some much-needed time off.

The new healthcare practitioners no longer have an interim place to work to sharpen their clinical skills, learn how to run a practice, and become more accomplished clinicians. Most new graduates start by applying for business loans to try and open a (very low budget) office. Often loaded with massive school loans, they typically won't qualify for additional debt, so the reality is that many are stuck working a couple of part time jobs, trying to save enough money to eventually start their own practice.

Good News for Everyone

There is good news all around for both senior healthcare practitioners and new graduates alike who follow Michael's principles and take my advice to heart. The multi-billion dollar all-cash nutrition market is experiencing double digit growth every year with no end in sight. Consumers are walking into retail vitamin chains and dropping large amounts of hard-earned cash on nutrition products sold by minimum wage sales clerks that may have been pumping gas the day before.

The people who are willing to do this are those who have decided to take charge of their own health and want something natural to assist them in their quest for wellness. Without a doubt, these same folks are patients like yours who would much prefer that their healthcare practitioners help direct their decision on what nutrition was best for them. However, since a lot of healthcare practitioners don't offer that service, these patients have no choice but to go the retail route.

Visionary healthcare practitioners who understand the dynamics of this consumer-driven self-medicating growth market are taking full advantage by opening nutrition profit centers and making plans to hire associate healthcare practitioners.

Insurance Reimbursement is Not Coming Back

Too many healthcare practitioners continue to sing the blues about insurance reimbursement loss. We healthcare practitioners need to accept the fact that insurance is not coming back so we can move on and become true entrepreneurs. We have Michael Gerber to show us the way to entrepreneurial nirvana, so what are we waiting for?

Nutrition is the golden ring that not only helps patients get well naturally, but it's also something that consumers want to buy from you. They are proving this by purchasing billions of dollars worth of nutrition products each and every month. You'll be able to capitalize on this new paradigm when you teach your people how to implement and fully operate your nutrition system.

An associate healthcare practitioner should be the keystone of this system, as he or she will fulfill all the same duties as associates have done in the past, but will also follow a proven system that will help expand your nutrition profit center into a nutrition business.

The Nutrition Business

Now that you've decided to employ an associate, you must be sure to hire the right person. Hiring a new healthcare practitioner right out of school who is loaded with clinical skills and nutritional experience can be difficult, so you must define exactly what your expectations are so your associate can follow your acceptable standards of care.

This hiring process not only sets a high standard of skill that you'll expect from your associate doctor, but it will also raise the overall standards for your nutrition profit center. As always, you need to keep an eye on the future and realize that the associate you hire will set the tone for the professionalism and financial stability of your practice. This is how you begin building a powerful nutrition profit center that can operate exactly as you expect it to.

New Opportunities with Associates

With all of this potential, you should view the selection of an associate as an opportunity to grow your nutrition profit center. As you define the standards you expect from your associate, you must also develop a system and action plan that outline exactly what you require from this person. The plan should include all necessary nutritional benchmarks, accountabilities, and budgets that your associate will be responsible for in operating the nutrition business.

To prepare for hiring an associate, be sure to clearly diagram the process you will follow to recruit, interview, train, manage, compensate, review, and terminate or reward the nutrition associate for his or her performance. All of these things need to be written out and placed in your nutrition profit center operating manual so your system is crystal clear to you and your associates. Once all of this is in place, all that's left for you to do is follow your plan to build your successful nutrition business.

We've covered people, and now associates; it's time to move on to the very important topic of estimating time in your business. ❧

CHAPTER 13

On the Subject of Estimating

Michael E. Gerber

The best we can do is size up the chances, calculate the risks involved, estimate our ability to deal with them, and then make our plans with confidence.

—Henry Ford

One of the greatest weaknesses of healthcare practitioners is accurately estimating how long appointments will take and then scheduling their patients accordingly. *Webster's Eleventh* defines estimate as "a rough or approximate calculation." Anyone who has visited a waiting room knows that those estimates can be rough indeed.

Do you want to see someone who gives you a rough approximation? What if your healthcare practitioner gave you a rough approximation of your condition?

The fact is that we can predict many things we don't typically predict. For example, there are ways to learn the truth about people who come in complaining about stomach irritability or acid reflux. Look at the steps of the process. Most of the things you do are standard, so develop a step-by-step system and stick to it.

In my book *The E-Myth Manager*, I raised eyebrows by suggesting that medical doctors eliminate the waiting room. Why? You don't need it if you're always on time. The same goes for a healthcare practice. If you're always on time, then your patients don't have to wait.

What if a healthcare practitioner made this promise: on time, every time, as promised, or we pay for it.

"Impossible!" healthcare practitioners cry. "Each patient is different. We simply can't know how long each appointment will take."

Do you follow this? Since healthcare practitioners believe they're incapable of knowing how to organize their time, they build a practice based on lack of knowing and lack of control. They build a practice based on estimates.

I once had a chiropractor ask me, "What happens when someone comes in for a routine adjustment and we discover they were diagnosed with a serious illness since their last visit? How can we deal with someone so unexpected? How can we give proper care and stay on schedule?"

My first thought was that it's not being dealt with now. Few healthcare practitioners are able to give generously of their time. Ask anyone who's been to a doctor's office lately. It's chaos.

The solution is interest, attention, analysis. Try detailing what you do at the beginning of an interaction, what you do in the middle, and what you do at the end. How long does each take? In the absence of such detailed, quantified standards, everything ends up being an estimate, and a poor estimate at that.

However, a practice organized around a system, with adequate staff to run it, has time for proper attention. It's built right into the system.

Too many healthcare practitioners have grown accustomed to thinking in terms of estimates without thinking about what the term really means. Is it any wonder many practices are in trouble?

Enlightened healthcare practitioners, in contrast, banish the word estimate from their vocabulary. When it comes to estimating, just say no!

"But you can never be exact," healthcare practitioners have told me for years. "Close, maybe. But never exact."

I have a simple answer to that: You have to be. You simply can't afford to be inexact. You can't accept inexactness in yourself or in your practice.

You can't go to work every day believing that your practice, the work you do, and the commitments you make are all too complex and unpredictable to be exact. With a mindset like that, you're doomed to run a sloppy ship. A ship that will eventually sink and suck you down with it.

This is so easy to avoid. Sloppiness—in both thought and action—is the root cause of your frustrations.

The solution to those frustrations is clarity. Clarity gives you the ability to set a clear direction, which fuels the momentum you need to grow your business.

Clarity, direction, momentum—they all come from insisting on exactness.

But how do you create exactness in a hopelessly inexact world? The answer is this. You discover the exactness in your practice by refusing to do any work that can't be controlled exactly.

The only other option is to analyze the market, determine where the opportunities are, and then organize your practice to be the exact practitioner of the services you've chosen to offer.

Two choices, and only two choices: (1) evaluate your practice and then limit yourself to the tasks you know you can do exactly, or (2) start all over by analyzing the market, identifying the key opportunities in that market, and building a practice that operates exactly.

What you cannot do, what you must refuse to do, from this day forward, is to allow yourself to operate with an inexact mindset. It will lead you to ruin.

Which leads us inexorably back to the word I have been using through this book: systems.

Who makes estimates? Only healthcare practitioners who are unclear about exactly how to do the task in question. Only healthcare practitioners whose experience has taught them that if something can go wrong, it will—and to them!

I'm not suggesting that a systems solution will guarantee that you always perform exactly as promised. But I am saying that a systems solution will faithfully alert you when you're going off track, and will do it before you have to pay the price for it.

In short, with a systems solution in place, your need to estimate will be a thing of the past, both because you have organized your practice to anticipate mistakes, and because you have put into place the system to do something about those mistakes before they blow up.

There's this, too: To make a promise you intend to keep places a burden on you and your managers to dig deeply into how you intend to keep it. Such a burden will transform your intentions and increase your attention to detail.

With the promise will come dedication. With dedication will come integrity. With integrity will come consistency. With consistency will come results you can count on. And results you can count on mean that you get exactly what you hoped for at the outset of your practice: the true pride of ownership that every healthcare practitioner should experience.

This brings us to the subject of patients. Who are they? Why do they come to you? How can you identify yours? And who should your patients be? But first, let's see what Dr. Hayes has to say about estimating. ✤

CHAPTER 14

Stay On Schedule, It's Essential

Dr. Donald L. Hayes, DC

A lot affects the outcome. It boils down to scheduling and the commitment of the network.

—David Ogden Stiers

Why are healthcare practitioners always behind schedule? It doesn't seem to matter what the specialty—it's a given that a patient's scheduled appointment time will not be honored. Michael's last chapter exposed why so many healthcare practitioners are suffering from a practice that is out of control. Disorganization is so rampant in healthcare today that most healthcare practitioners and patients alike don't even seem to notice that they're always behind schedule; it's just something that everyone seems to accept, as inescapable as gravity. It takes a real pioneer like Michael to step forward and say to healthcare practitioners, enough! Enough indifference, enough disorganization, enough being late, enough, enough, enough!

As I write this chapter, I'm reminded of my own years in private practice before I implemented the E-Myth principles, and I realize how much time I cost all of my patients by being late and disorganized. It was simply not right! Yet healthcare practitioners today are still working from the same old paradigm and operating on the same old late schedules.

So if I'm going to educate you about using nutrition supplements in your practice, and demonstrate to you how to make it a huge financial success, I have to address this issue of Estimating and illustrate what you must do in this regard in order to have any chance of growth.

Healthcare Practitioners Must Get Organized

First, all healthcare practitioners have to get their private practice acts together. There's simply no excuse for any of us to be so disorganized and behind schedule. The only reason we accept it in our practices is because it's the way every other healthcare practitioner does it, and for some reason patients continue to go along with it. But once you see how big a difference being organized will make in the lives of your patients, and how it can make a gigantic increase in your practice income, I know you'll agree to change in a New York minute!

Michael makes a huge E-Myth observation on how important it is that your business is different than other businesses just like yours. Can you imagine how much you would stand out from other doctors if you had a reputation of always being on time? Remember, no matter how impossible you think it is for you to be on time, Michael is adamant that you make it happen, and he's given you two ways to do it. You must either limit your tasks to what you know you can do on time, or start a new practice from scratch and build it to operate on time.

The decision is up to you, but let me make one point perfectly clear: If you're chronically late as a healthcare practitioner, you have to stop and change that behavior immediately because it's killing your reputation, leveling your patient satisfaction and drastically limiting your new patient referrals. You must use the E-Myth principles to get and stay on schedule in your regular practice.

Offering nutrition to patients within your practice must be done using a system and it must be done on time. You can't afford to take time away from your already busy practice with added confusion and disorganization around what isolated nutrient or vitamin supplement works best for each patient.

The Nutrition Slow Down

By now you know how I feel about Condition Specific Nutrition. As a healthcare practitioner myself who has consulted in some of the most successful nutrition profit centers in the world, I must say it's nearly impossible for any of us to determine with complete certainty the exact nutrient a patient needs. Offering nutrition in your practice one bottle at a time, using a "this for that" approach, simply means that you are spending way too much time trying to figure out what nutrient is the perfect fit for each patient's particular symptom or health challenge.

When you combine that method with the fact that most of the large nutrition companies now have 500-to-800 different types of nutrients, you'll be quickly overwhelmed when it comes to recommending nutritional products, and you'll be wasting valuable time. If this is the way you currently practice nutrition, you need to take Michael's advice and consider starting a new nutrition profit center from scratch so you can build it to operate on time.

A Better Solution

There is a direct opposite school of thought from offering one bottle at a time, and that is providing Whole Body Alkaline Nutritional support to all patients on their first visit. This is an umbrella approach to nutrition that will benefit every patient, regardless of their health challenge. Products should focus on providing as much whole food supplementation as possible to support a healthy inflammatory response, manage the acid-alkaline pH balance of the body, and help facilitate proper muscle function and repair of connective tissue.

This type of nutritional approach follows the research outlined by many leading scientists, which shows that the body should be given as much whole food as possible with a minimum of isolated vitamins or minerals. When the body is given what it recognizes, which is whole food (easily offered in your practice as a whole food powdered supplement that contains all three food groups), it will metabolize what it needs and discard the rest.

Only the body really knows what it needs at any given time. As healthcare practitioners recommending nutrition to our patients, it makes complete sense that when we provide the body the essential forty micronutrients derived from whole foods that consist of the three food groups—complex carbohydrates, plant-based protein and healthy essential oils—the wisdom of the body will select and utilize exactly what it needs.

This is not to say that as healthcare practitioners, we should not also recommend specific targeted nutrients for specific conditions, but this broad approach to nutritional support may help more people while also saving us a lot of time.

Your only concern, of course, should be helping patients, and you can absolutely accomplish that with this type of nutritional approach which is less complicated, less of a burden on your overhead, and less time consuming for you and your office staff.

In short, with a nutrition system in place, your practice habit of always being chronically late will disappear. The system will help you to better estimate your time, help keep the practice organized, and help you avoid mistakes. Instead of each person doing their own thing, which just contributes to practice chaos, you and your staff will simply follow the system.

At this point, you've learned about how to best utilize the people in your business, but of course we know that the people on your team are only one part of the equation of your practice—the other being, of course, your patients. Now seems the perfect time to see what Michael has to say about dealing with patients in your practice. ✤

On the Subject
of Patients

Michael E. Gerber

*Some clients I see are actually draining into their bodies the diseased
thoughts of their minds.*

—Zachary T. Bercovitz, *Wisdom for the Soul:*
Five Millennia of Prescriptions for Spiritual Healing

W hen it comes to healthcare, the best definition of
patients I've ever heard is this:
Patients: *very special people who drive most healthcare
practitioners crazy.*

Does that work for you?

After all, it's a rare patient who shows any appreciation for what
a healthcare practitioner has to go through to do the job as promised. Don't they always think the price is too high? And don't they
focus on problems, broken promises, and the mistakes they think you
make, rather than all the ways you bend over backward to give them
what they need?

Do you ever hear other healthcare practitioners voice these complaints? More to the point, have you ever voiced them yourself? Well, you're not alone. I have yet to meet a healthcare practitioner who doesn't suffer from a strong case of patient confusion.

Patient confusion is about:

- what your patient really wants;
- how to communicate effectively with your patient;
- how to keep your patient happy;
- how to deal with patient dissatisfaction; and
- whom to call a patient.

Confusion 1: What Your Patient Really Wants

Your patients aren't just people; they're very specific kinds of people. Let me share with you the six categories of patients as seen from the E-Myth marketing perspective: (1) tactile patients, (2) neutral patients, (3) withdrawal patients, (4) experimental patients, (5) transitional patients, and (6) traditional patients.

Your entire marketing strategy must be based on which type of patient you are dealing with. Each of the six patient types spends money on healthcare services for very different, and identifiable, reasons. These are:

- Tactile patients get their major gratification from interacting with other people.
- Neutral patients get their major gratification from interacting with inanimate objects (computers, cars, information).
- Withdrawal patients get their major gratification from interacting with ideas (thoughts, concepts, stories).
- Experimental patients rationalize their buying decisions by perceiving that what they bought is new, revolutionary, and innovative.

- Transitional patients rationalize their buying decisions by perceiving that what they bought is dependable and reliable.
- Traditional patients rationalize their buying decisions by perceiving that what they bought is cost-effective, a good deal, and worth the money.

In short:

- If your patient is tactile, you have to emphasize the *people* of your practice.
- If your patient is neutral, you have to emphasize the *technology* of your practice.
- If your patient is a withdrawal client, you have to emphasize the *idea* of your practice.
- If your patient is experimental, you have to emphasize the *uniqueness* of your practice.
- If your patient is transitional, you have to emphasize the *dependability* of your practice.
- If your patient is traditional, you have to talk about the *financial competitiveness* of your practice.

What your patients want is determined by who they are. Who they are is regularly demonstrated by what they do. Think about the patients with whom you do business. Ask yourself: In which of the categories would I place them? What do they do for a living?

If your patient is a mechanical engineer, for example, it's probably safe to assume he's a neutral patient. If another one of your patients is a cardiologist, she's probably tactile. Accountants tend to be traditional, and software engineers are often experimental.

Having an idea about which categories your patients may fall into is very helpful to figuring out what they want. Of course, there's no exact science to it, and human beings constantly defy stereotypes. So don't take my word for it. You'll want to make your own analysis of the patients you serve.

Confusion 2: How to Communicate Effectively with Your Patient

The next step in the patient satisfaction process is to decide how to magnify the characteristics of your practice that are most likely to appeal to your preferred category of patient. That begins with what marketing people call your *positioning strategy*.

What do I mean by *positioning* your practice? You position your practice with words. A few well-chosen words to tell your patients exactly what they want to hear. In marketing lingo, those words are called your USP, or unique selling proposition.

For example, if you are targeting tactile patients (ones who love people), your USP could be: "Wellness Care, where the feelings of people *really* count!"

If you are targeting experimental patients (ones who love new, revolutionary things), your USP could be: "Wellness Care, where living on the edge is a way of life!" In other words, when they choose to schedule an appointment with you, they can count on both your services and equipment to be on the cutting edge of the industry.

Is this starting to make sense? Do you see how the ordinary things most healthcare practitioners do to get patients can be done in a significantly more effective way?

Once you understand the essential principles of marketing the E-Myth way, the strategies by which you attract patients can make an enormous difference in your market share.

Confusion 3: How to Keep Your Patient Happy

Let's say you've overcome the first two confusions. Great. Now how do you keep your patient happy?

Very simple . . . just keep your promise! And make sure your patient *knows* you kept your promise every step of the way.

In short, giving your patients what they think they want is the key to keeping your patients (or anyone else, for that matter) really happy.

If your patients need to interact with people (high touch, tactile), make certain that they do.

If they need to interact with things (high-tech, neutral), make certain that they do.

If they need to interact with ideas (in their head, withdrawal), make certain that they do.

And so forth.

At E-Myth, we call this your *patient fulfillment system*. It's the step-by-step process by which you do the task you've contracted to do and deliver what you've promised—on time, every time.

But what happens when your patients are *not* happy? What happens when you've done everything I've mentioned here and your patient is still dissatisfied?

Confusion 4: How to Deal with Patient Dissatisfaction

If you have followed each step up to this point, patient dissatisfaction will be rare. But it can and will still occur—people are people, and some people will always find a way to be dissatisfied with something. Here's what to do about it:

- Always listen to what your patients are saying. And never interrupt while they're saying it.

- After you're sure you've heard all of your patient's complaint, make absolutely certain you understand what she said by phrasing a question, such as: "Can I repeat what you've just told me, Ms. Harton, to make absolutely certain I understand you?"

- Secure your patient's acknowledgment that you have heard her complaint accurately.

- Apologize for whatever your patient thinks you did that dissatisfied her, even if you didn't do it!

- After your patient has acknowledged your apology, ask her exactly what would make her happy.

- Repeat what your patient told you would make her happy, and get her acknowledgment that you have heard correctly.
- If at all possible, give your patient exactly what she has asked for.

You may be thinking, "But what if my patient wants something totally impossible?" Don't worry. If you've followed my recommendations to the letter, what your patient asks for will seldom seem unreasonable.

Confusion 5: Whom to Call a Patient

At this stage, it's important to ask yourself some questions about the kind of patients you hope to attract to your practice:

- Which types of patients would you most like to do business with?
- Where do you see your real market opportunities?
- Who would you like to work with, provide services to, and position your business for?

In short, *it's all up to you*. No mystery. No magic. Just a systematic process for shaping your practice's future. But you must have the passion to pursue the process. And you must be absolutely clear about every aspect of it.

Until you know your patients as well as you know yourself.

Until all your complaints about patients are a thing of the past.

Until you accept the undeniable fact that patient acquisition and patient satisfaction are more science than art.

But unless you're willing to grow your practice, you'd better not follow any of these recommendations. Because if you do what I'm suggesting, it's going to grow.

This brings us to the subject of growth. But first, let's see what Dr. Hayes has to say about patients. ❧

16

Give Patients What They Want

Dr. Donald L. Hayes, DC

The main way you learn in medicine is by practicing and working with patients.

—Andrew Weil

It seems so simple, doesn't it? Just give patients what they want! You know the old adage: the customer is always right. Why, then, do so many healthcare practitioners, whether or not they use nutrition, violate this most basic and sacred common sense rule?

I want to elaborate on confusion number one from Michael's list of the five types of patient confusion—what your patients really want—because if you're going to grow a successful nutrition profit center, you've got to clear that confusion up fast!

I keep thinking of Michael's statement that patients go to healthcare practitioners for the right reasons—their pain, their condition, and their circumstance. The pain they have is a real concern for them, and they want a healthcare practitioner to help them relieve it.

You know by now that most people are able and willing to pay for the things they "want," but not always for the things they "need," so with that in mind, let me elaborate on what I've learned is the single biggest thing that patients want and will pay for.

Patients Want Relief as Soon as Possible

This isn't hard to understand. Patients go to you to get relief from their personal health challenges and they want them gone as quickly as possible. With that in mind, a recommendation that combines your primary treatment with Whole Body Alkaline Nutrition will most likely be embraced by a majority of patients because it can significantly improve their rate of healing and lessen the time needed for recovery.

It's very important that you select nutrition products that are designed to support a healthy inflammatory response and help manage the acid-alkaline pH balance of the body. In addition, the nutrition products you recommend should provide an easy way for patients to fuel their healthy, active lifestyle.

Homeostasis, Allostasis and Allostatic Load

In his landmark book *The Wisdom of the Body*, Walter Cannon, M.D. coined the medical term "homeostasis" and established the basis for internal pH balance, inflammation, and the medical field of neuroendocrinology.

Cannon graduated summa cum laude from Harvard and was a professor of physiology at Harvard Medical School for over twenty years. He postulated that in order for the body to maintain health, it could only do so by achieving homeostasis, which, in its simplest form, means balance.

Cannon indicated that homeostasis is controlled and maintained by two distinct channels in the body: the electrical channel of the nervous system and the chemical channel of the endocrine system.

This field of study, known as neuroendocrinology, deals with the interactions between the nervous system (the master system of the body) and the endocrine system (the series of glands that release the hormones that direct most of the body's activities).

Bad lifestyle choices like poor diet, lack of exercise, smoking, and many others, challenge the homeostasis, or balance, in the body. Two new terms were created in the scientific literature to explain these lifestyle-stressor-caused responses: allostasis and allostatic load.

Allostasis is defined as "maintaining homeostasis through change." Allostatic load refers to a state where lifestyle stressors have accumulated to the point that they affect homeostasis and create symptoms.

While at Harvard, Cannon taught Arthur Guyton, M.D., who went on to become arguably the greatest physiologist the world has ever known. Guyton wrote *The Textbook of Medical Physiology*, which is still used today in most healthcare practitioner schools. In the book, Guyton established normal body fluid pH ranges from 6.0 to 7.4, whole blood at a range of pH 7.35 to 7.45, arterial blood at a pH of 7.4, venous blood at a pH of 7.35, average urine pH at 6.0, and the high end for saliva pH at 7.4. He dedicated Chapter 37, entitled "Maintaining Homeostasis: Regulation of Acid-Base Balance" to his mentor, Cannon.

Guyton expounded greatly on the importance of maintaining homeostasis and a healthy acid-alkaline balance, and how those directly relate to chronic inflammation:

- "The first step in maintaining health is to alkalize the body."
- "The cells of a healthy body are alkaline, while the cells of a diseased body are below a pH of 7.0. The more acidic the cell, the sicker we become."
- "Since our bodies do not manufacture alkalinity, we must supply the alkalinity from an outside source to keep from becoming acidic and dying."

Remember that patients are coming in to see if you can offer a natural alternative to relieve their symptoms. You're going to significantly increase your patients' health if you offer Whole Body Alkaline Nutrition that focuses on maintaining homeostasis in conjunction with your routine treatments.

Patients Always Have a Secondary Want

We've established that patients primarily want relief from their main complaint, but if you ask a few questions and dig a little deeper, you will find what I call the patient's "secondary want." This is tied to their health goal, and it's another reason they want to get out of pain.

For instance, golfers want to play golf, fitness enthusiasts want to exercise, parents want to play with their kids, grandparents want to lift their grandchildren, and on and on. If you are curious and ask the right questions, you can find a patient's secondary reason for visiting your office, and many times, that reason is an even bigger motivator for them than just getting quick relief. Again, by providing Whole Body Alkaline Nutrition along with your regular treatments, you will more than likely enable your patients to attain their secondary want much more quickly.

The Easiest Way to Recommend Whole Body Alkaline Nutrition

I was talking to one of my very successful nutrition profit center clients recently, a dermatologist who recommends one of my products to all of her patients. I asked her what her secret was to selling so much of the fruit and vegetable superfood drink mix and she gave me this answer:

"Dr. Hayes, you know as well as I do that excess acid in the body is stored in fat cells and under the skin. When enough acid accumulates under the skin it contributes to skin wrinkles and inflammation. I tell my patients that the dermatology treatments I use work on the outside of the skin and the alkalizing supplement

I recommend helps support the inflammatory process on the inside of your body."

Her explanation was so simple and so accurate, I told her that I was going to share it with other healthcare practitioners so they could use a version of it with their patients.

In the language of Dr. Cannon's vision of homeostasis and the field of neuroendocrinology, we can explain it this way: proper alkalizing nutrition, used in conjunction with body work designed to support the nervous system, can have a powerful effect on reducing the allostatic load and returning the body to homeostasis.

How to Give Patients What They Want

Do you want your practice to grow or not? If the answer is yes, then you need to do everything possible in the short-term to help your patients reach homeostasis as soon as possible. This is the best way to get more patients engaged in the value of health, and may actually get more of them to stick around long-term, giving you the opportunity to get them all the care you know they need.

Michael told us in the last chapter that he hasn't met a healthcare practitioner who doesn't suffer from a strong case of patient confusion. We're confused about what patients really want, confused about how to communicate effectively with them, confused about how to keep them happy, confused about how to deal properly with their dissatisfaction, and confused about how to attract the kinds of patients we want.

If you, as a healthcare practitioner, focus on correcting the first patient confusion, and start giving your patients what they really want, most (if not all) of your other confusions will begin to fade away and your practice will begin to grow.

Now let's turn to the topic of growth in your business. Growth, after all, is what any ambitious business owner desires, but the gap between ambition and growth is sometimes too far to clear. Michael bridges that gap with his own advice on growth in the practice in the next chapter. ❧

17

On the Subject of Growth

Michael E. Gerber

*As we learn we always change, and so our perception. This changed
perception then becomes a new Teacher inside each of us.*

—Hyemeyohsts Storm

The rule of business growth says that every business, like every
child, is destined to grow. Needs to grow. Is determined to grow.

Once you've created your practice, once you've shaped
the idea of it, the most natural thing for it to do is to . . . grow! And if
you stop it from growing, it will die.

Once a healthcare practitioner has started a practice, it's his or
her job to help it grow. To nurture it and support it in every way. To
infuse it with

- Purpose;
- Passion;
- Will;

111

- Belief;
- Personality; and
- Method.

As your practice grows, it naturally changes. And as it changes from a small practice to something much bigger, you will begin to feel out of control. News flash: that's because you *are* out of control.

Your practice *has* exceeded your know-how, sprinted right past you, and now it's taunting you to keep up. That leaves you two choices: grow as big as your practice demands you grow, or try to hold your practice at its present level—at the level you feel most comfortable.

The sad fact is that most healthcare practitioners do the latter. They try to keep their practice small, securely within their comfort zone. Doing what they know how to do, what they feel most comfortable doing. It's called playing it safe.

But as the practice grows, the number, scale, and complexity of tasks will grow, too, until they threaten to overwhelm the healthcare practitioner. More people are needed. More space. More money. Everything seems to be happening at the same time. A hundred balls are in the air at once.

As I've said throughout this book: Most healthcare practitioners are not entrepreneurs. They aren't true businesspeople at all, but technicians suffering from an entrepreneurial seizure. Their philosophy of coping with the workload can be summarized as "just do it," rather than figuring out how to get it done through other people using innovative systems to produce consistent results.

Given most healthcare practitioners' inclination to be the master juggler in their practice, it's not surprising that as complexity increases, as work expands beyond their ability to do it, as money becomes more elusive, they are just holding on, desperately juggling more and more balls. In the end, most collapse under the strain.

You can't expect your practice to stand still. You can't expect your practice to stay small. A practice that stays small and depends on you to do everything isn't a practice—it's a job!

Yes, just like your children, your business must be allowed to grow, to flourish, to change, to become more than it is. In this way, it will match your vision. And you know all about vision, right? You'd better. It's what you do best!

Do you feel the excitement? You should. After all, you know what your practice *is* but not what it *can be*.

It's either going to grow or die. The choice is yours, but it is a choice that must be made. If you sit back and wait for change to overtake you, you will always have to answer no to this question: Are you ready?

This brings us to the subject of *change*. But first, let's see what Dr. Hayes has to say about growth. ♣

Automate to Grow

Dr. Donald L. Hayes, DC

Without continual growth and progress, such words as improvement,
achievement, and success have no meaning.

—Benjamin Franklin

Consider this: "In all of nature nothing stays the same; you're either striving to make yourself better, or allowing yourself to get worse."

Too many healthcare practitioners are allowing their practices to get worse by letting the practice run them instead of the other way around. They're slaves to their businesses, they're putting in lots of clinic hours, and they're dealing with tons of financial stress that negatively impacts their health, their lifestyle, and their family.

How is it that upon graduating from school we feel so much excitement and joy about opening our own practice, and then, within an all too short period of time, we become overwhelmed, disillusioned, bitter, exhausted, scared, and we wonder, "Where did I go wrong?"

There's no doubt that this thing you call a practice, your business, is very important, but you can't make it more important than your life. In order to prevent this from happening, you have to first be aware of it, and then you must put systems in place to prevent your practice from taking over your life.

Your practice is meant to grow; if it doesn't, it will die. And as it begins to die, so do you, by shouldering a little more stress each day. So how do we fix this problem? How do we figure out how to have both a very fulfilling life and an outrageously successful practice? Here's how.

The No Inventory Online Nutrition Store

If you want to generate a solid income stream from nutrition, find a nutrition company that will host and maintain an automated online store for your practice. The entire process should be hassle-free and require no inventory; that way, all you have to do is refer your patients to your web store where they can purchase your nutrition products. Make sure you use a system that will fulfill all orders for you and provide you with the full wholesale margins that you are entitled to as a healthcare practitioner.

This type of automated online store is perfect for healthcare practitioners who want to offer nutrition in their practice but:

- Don't have the time.
- Don't want to stock any products in their office.
- Don't want the hassle of fulfilling orders.
- Don't want to tie up valuable staff time selling a lot of products.

How an Online Nutrition Store Works

Nutrition companies typically only offer an online nutrition store to licensed healthcare practitioners who have decided to offer that company's nutrition products to their patients and with whom they have a wholesale agreement.

The nutrition company you choose should create a simple user-friendly website which will become your very own online nutrition store where you can send patients and other customers to purchase the products you offer. The nutrition company should also:

- Include all product images.
- Provide complete descriptions of each product.
- Handle all of the required website security certificates.
- Include an "AutoShip" option for patients to receive product on an ongoing basis.
- Manage complete fulfillment of all products ordered.

Furthermore, this type of online nutrition store should give you administrative access to your web store where you can:

- Customize key content on your website.
- Set the prices you want to charge for each product.
- Set the shipping charges patients will pay.

Typically, you will need to set up some type of credit card payment account system to be able to accept payment from your patients. Once that is established, and the web store is up and running, there should be very little administrative work required to maintain the site. Here's how easy it should be:

When you recommend a specific nutrition product to your patient, the patient will go to your online nutrition store to place their order. The patient will pay via a major credit card with the payment going directly to you, the doctor. When the nutrition company receives the order for fulfillment from your website, it will charge the credit card you have on file with them for the wholesale cost of the order. The nutrition company will fulfill the order and ship the products directly to your patient, and the patient will be notified that a third party is fulfilling the order.

That's it! And all without any website management or maintenance cost to you. In fact, the only cost should be the fee that the credit card company charges for their services, and this should be disclosed to you prior to you deciding to sign up.

A no-inventory online nutrition store is congruent with the E-Myth principles because it's simple, automated, predictable, and profitable. There's no better way to grow your practice profits, and at the same time ensure that your patients get the ongoing nutritional support they need.

We're beginning to put all of the puzzle pieces together on how to build a successful practice. With success comes change, which leads us to Michael's next chapter on how to navigate that change. ✤

On the Subject of Change

Michael E. Gerber

There is nothing permanent except change.
—Diogenes Laërtius, *Lives of the Philosophers*

S o your practice is growing. That means, of course, that it's also changing. Which means it's driving you and everyone in your life crazy.

I've talked to countless healthcare practitioners whose hopes weren't being realized through their practice; whose lives were consumed by work; who slaved increasingly longer hours for decreasing pay; whose dissatisfaction grew as their enjoyment shriveled; whose practice had become the worst job in the world; whose money was out of control; whose employees were a source of never-ending hassles, just like their patients, their bank, and, increasingly, even their families.

More and more, these healthcare practitioners spent their time alone, dreading the unknown and anxious about the future. And even when they were with people, they didn't know how to relax. Their mind was always on the job. They were distracted by work, by the thought of work. By the fear of falling behind.

And yet, when confronted with their condition and offered an alternative, most of the same healthcare practitioners strenuously resisted. They assumed that if there were a better way of doing business, they already would have figured it out. They derived comfort from knowing what they believed they already knew. They accepted the limitations of being a healthcare practitioner; or the truth about people; or the limitations of what they could expect from their patients, their employees, their associate healthcare practitioner, their bankers—even their family and friends.

In short, most healthcare practitioner I've met over the years would rather live with the frustrations they already have than risk enduring new frustrations.

Isn't that true of most people you know? Rather than opening up to the infinite number of possibilities life offers, they prefer to shut their life down to respectable limits. After all, isn't that the most reasonable way to live?

I think not. I think we must learn to let go. I think that if you fail to embrace change, it will inevitably destroy you.

Conversely, by opening yourself to change, you give your practice the opportunity to get the most from your talents.

Let me share with you an original way to think about change, about life, about who we are and what we do. About the stunning notion of expansion and contraction.

Contraction vs. Expansion

"Our salvation," a wise man once said, "is to allow." That is, to be open, to let go of our beliefs, to change. Only then can we move from a point of view to a viewing point.

That wise man was Thaddeus Golas, the author of a small, powerful book entitled *The Lazy Man's Guide to Enlightenment* (Seed Center, 1971).

Among the many inspirational things he had to say was this compelling idea:

The basic function of each being is expanding and contracting. Expanded beings are permeative; contracted beings are dense and impermeative. Therefore each of us, alone or in combination, may appear as space, energy, or mass, depending on the ratio of expansion to contraction chosen, and what kind of vibrations each of us expresses by alternating expansion and contraction. Each being controls his own vibrations.

In other words, Golas tells us that the entire mystery of life can be summed up in two words: *expansion* and *contraction*. He goes on to say:

We experience expansion as awareness, comprehension, understanding, or whatever we wish to call it.

When we are completely expanded, we have a feeling of total awareness, of being one with all life.

At that level we have no resistance to any vibrations or interactions of other beings. It is timeless bliss, with unlimited choice of consciousness, perception, and feeling.

When a [human] being is totally contracted, he is a mass particle, completely imploded.

To the degree that he is contracted, a being is unable to be in the same space with others, so contraction is felt as fear, pain, unconsciousness, ignorance, hatred, evil, and a whole host of strange feelings.

At an extreme [of contraction, a human being] has the feeling of being completely insane, of resisting everyone and everything, of being unable to choose the content of his consciousness.

Of course, these are just the feelings appropriate to mass vibration levels, and he can get out of them at any time by expanding, by letting go of all resistance to what he thinks, sees, or feels.

Stay with me here. Because what Golas says is profoundly important. When you're feeling oppressed, overwhelmed, exhausted by more than you can control—contracted, as Golas puts it—you can change your state to one of expansion.

According to Golas, the more contracted we are, the more threatened by change; the more expanded we are, the more open to change.

In our most enlightened—that is, open—state, change is as welcome as non-change. Everything is perceived as a part of ourselves. There is no inside or outside. Everything is one thing. Our sense of isolation is transformed to a feeling of ease, of light, of joyful relationship with everything.

As infants, we didn't even think of change in the same way, because we lived those first days in an unthreatened state. Insensitive to the threat of loss, most young children are only aware of *what is*. Change is simply another form of *what is*. Change just *is*.

However, when we are in our most contracted—that is, closed—state, change is the most extreme threat. If the known is what I have, then the unknown must be what threatens to take away what I have. Change, then, is the unknown. And the unknown is fear. It's like being between trapezes.

- To the fearful, change is threatening because things may get worse.

- To the hopeful, change is encouraging because things may get better.

- To the confident, change is inspiring because the challenge exists to improve things.

If you are fearful, you see difficulties in every opportunity. If you are fear-free, you see opportunities in every difficulty.

Fear protects what I have from being taken away. But it also disconnects me from the rest of the world. In other words, fear keeps me separate and alone.

Here's the exciting part of Golas's message: with this new understanding of contraction and expansion, we can become completely attuned to where we are at all times.

If I am afraid, suspicious, skeptical, and resistant, I am in a contracted state. If I am joyful, open, interested, and willing, I am in an expanded state. Just knowing this puts me on an expanded path. Always remembering this, Golas says, brings enlightenment, which opens me even more.

Such openness gives me the ability to freely access my options. And taking advantage of options is the best part of change. Just as there are infinite ways to greet a client, there are infinite ways to run your company. If you believe Thaddeus Golas, your most exciting option is to be open to all of them.

Because your life is lived on a continuum between the most contracted and most expanded—the most closed and most open—states, change is best understood as the movement from one to the other, and back again.

Most small-business owners I've met see change as a thing in itself, as something that just happens to them. Most experience change as a threat. Whenever change shows up at the door, they quickly slam it. Many bolt the door and pile up the furniture. Some even run for their gun.

Few of them understand that change isn't a thing in itself, but rather the manifestation of many things. You might call it the revelation of all possibilities. Think of it as the ability at any moment to sacrifice what we are for what we could become.

Change can either challenge us or threaten us. It's our choice. Our attitude toward change can either pave the way to success or throw up a roadblock.

Change is where opportunity lives. Without change we would stay exactly as we are. The universe would be frozen still. Time would end.

At any given moment, we are somewhere on the path between a contracted and expanded state. Most of us are in the middle of the journey, neither totally closed nor totally open. According to Golas, change is our movement from one place in the middle toward one of the two ends.

Do you want to move toward contraction or toward enlightenment? Because without change, you are hopelessly stuck with what you've got.

Without change,

- we have no hope;
- we cannot know true joy;

- we will not get better; and
- we will continue to focus exclusively on what we have and the threat of losing it.

All of this negativity contracts us even more, until, at the extreme closed end of the spectrum, we become a black hole so dense that no light can get in or out.

Sadly, the harder we try to hold on to what we've got, the less able we are to do so. So we try still harder, which eventually drags us even deeper into the black hole of contraction.

Are you like that? Do you know anybody who is?

Think of change as the movement between where we are and where we're not. That leaves only two directions for change: either moving forward or slipping backward. We become either more contracted or more expanded.

The next step is to link change to how we feel. If we feel afraid, change is dragging us backward. If we feel open, change is pushing us forward.

Change is not a thing in itself, but a movement of our consciousness. By tuning in, by paying attention, we get clues to the state of our being.

Change, then, is not an outcome or something to be acquired. Change is a shift of our consciousness, of our being, of our humanity, of our attention, of our relationship with all other beings in the universe.

We are either "more in relationship" or "less in relationship." Change is the movement in either of those directions. The exciting part is that *we possess the ability to decide which way we go . . . and to know, in the moment, which way we're moving.*

Closed, open . . . Open, closed. Two directions in the universe. The choice is yours.

Do you see the profound opportunity available to you? What an extraordinary way to live!

Enlightenment is not reserved for the sainted. Rather, it comes to us as we become more sensitive to ourselves. Eventually, we become our own guides, alerting ourselves to our state, moment by moment: *open . . . closed . . . open . . . closed.*

Listen to your inner voice, your ally, and feel what it's like to be open and closed. Experience the instant of choice in both directions.

You will feel the awareness growing. It may be only a flash at first, so be alert. This feeling is accessible, but only if you avoid the black hole of contraction.

Are you afraid that you're totally contracted? Don't be—it's doubtful. The fact that you're still reading this book suggests that you're moving in the opposite direction.

You're more like a running back seeking the open field. You can see the opportunity gleaming in the distance. In the open direction.

Understand that I'm not saying that change itself is a point on the path; rather, it's the all-important movement.

Change is *in you*, not *out there*.

What path are you on? The path of liberation? Or the path of crystallization?

As we know, change can be for the better or for the worse.

If change is happening *inside* of you, it is for the worse only if you remain closed to it. The key, then, is your attitude—your acceptance or rejection of change. Change can be for the better only if you accept it. And it will certainly be for the worse if you don't.

Remember, change is nothing in itself. Without you, change doesn't exist. Change is happening inside of each of us, giving us clues to where we are at any point in time.

Rejoice in change, for it's a sign you are alive.

Are we open? Are we closed? If we're open, good things are bound to happen. If we're closed, things will only get worse.

According to Golas, it's as simple as that. Whatever happens defines where we are. *How* we are is *where* we are. It cannot be any other way.

For change is life.

Charles Darwin wrote, "It is not the strongest of the species that survive, nor the most intelligent, but the one that proves itself most responsive to change."

The growth of your healthcare practice, then, is its change. Your role is to go with it, to be with it, to share the joy, embrace the opportunities, meet the challenges, learn the lessons.

Remember, there are three kinds of people: (1) those who make things happen, (2) those who let things happen, and (3) those who wonder what the hell happened. The people who make things happen are masters of change. The other two are its victims.

Which type are you?

The Big Change

If all this is going to mean anything to the life of your practice, you have to know when you're going to leave it. At what point, in your practice's rise from where it is now to where it can ultimately grow, are you going to sell it? Because if you don't have a clear picture of when you want out, your practice is the master of your destiny, not the reverse.

As we stated earlier, the most valuable form of money is equity, and unless your business vision includes your equity and how you will use it to your advantage, you will forever be consumed by your practice.

Your practice is potentially the best friend you ever had. It is your practice's nature to serve you, so let it. If, however, you are not a wise steward, if you do not tell your practice what you expect from it, it will run rampant, abuse you, use you, and confuse you.

Change. Growth. Equity.

Focus on the point in the future when you will take leave of your practice. Now reconsider your goals in that context. Be specific. Write them down.

Skipping this step is like tiptoeing through earthquake country. Who can say where the fault lies waiting? And who knows exactly when your whole world may come crashing down around you?

Which brings us to the subject of *time*. But first, let's see what Dr. Hayes has to say about change. ✤

Embrace the Opportunity to Change

Dr. Donald L. Hayes, DC

They always say time changes things, but you actually have to change them yourself.

—Andy Warhol

M any changes are now occurring in the practices and lives of healthcare practitioners, but does "change" have to equal "crisis?" No. Not if you have the tools to positively change your situation, and that is what we're going to discuss in this chapter.

Let's face it, a lot of healthcare practitioners are in a state of shock today because of the changing state of healthcare, which includes the loss of insurance reimbursements, the relentless growth of managed care, and the continued slowing down of practice growth. Many doctors are frozen in a place of despair. Not wanting to make things worse, many choose to do nothing. They figure since change is responsible for their current problems, they had better just sit still and wait for it to get better on its own.

Michael said, "The growth of your practice is its change and your role is to go with it, to share the joy and embrace the opportunities." I can hear my colleagues saying in disbelief, "Are you kidding me? Embrace the opportunities? What opportunities? Things are worse than ever, and getting worse every day!"

This is a book about the business of nutrition, and I am confident that if you create a turnkey nutrition system to run your nutrition profit center and then add that nutrition profit center to your existing practice, you will be able to overcome most—if not all—challenging practice changes.

Let's examine some business facts. I have some good news and some bad news regarding three significant business changes that have occurred in the chiropractic profession over the past twenty years. Now, I realize that there are many healthcare practitioners reading this book who are not chiropractors, but typically what happens to one alternative healthcare profession also impacts the other ones.

In each of the three statistics I list below, I'm going to get the bad news out of the way first, discuss the impact that statistical change has had on the profession, and then come up with a solution on how we can deal with each change and turn it into a positive.

One last thing: the statistics I'm about to quote for you are not new. They've been out for many years and I would guess that most chiropractors are aware of them. However, like Michael said, what happens to many of us is that when we're confronted with bad changes (like these statistics represent) and then, offered an alternative solution, most of us resist. Whether this is your first time confronting these statistics or not, please do not resist the opportunity to change. Don't settle for living with your current frustrations just because you're afraid you'll get new ones. Make an agreement with yourself to take advantage of the opportunity and make positive changes.

Statistics on Chiropractic and Nutrition

The American Chiropractic Association (ACA) has been surveying its members on various aspects of the chiropractic profession for decades. Some of the data goes back to the 1960s, but the majority of it dates back about 30 years. And while the responses of the ACA members do not necessarily speak for the entire chiropractic profession, they're indicative of some interesting patterns of change.

1. Less New Patients to Chiropractors

The number of new patients to chiropractors decreased 25 percent over a seventeen-year period, from thirty-two per month in 1979 to twenty-four per month in 1996. A general consensus of chiropractors today would agree that a lack of new patients is still a substantial problem.

Impact of This Change

Chiropractors have to ask themselves why 25 percent fewer people are scheduling as new patients and figure out what they can do about it. Obviously, there are not fewer sick people in the world today, so maybe the answer is that every chiropractor on the planet needs to get out and tell the chiropractic story. Maybe they need to tell everyone they meet what chiropractic is all about and how it can help. In the long-term, this process can do tremendous good. But in the short-term they need to immediately put into place a turnkey marketing system to turn this statistic around.

Nutrition during the same seventeen-year time period has exploded in growth. It seems only logical that the marketing message you employ (be it chiropractic or any other discipline) should tell all patients that you use nutritional supplementation as part of your protocols so you can participate in the same wave of growth and give patients the key alkalizing nutrients they need.

2. Gross and Net Income Down for Chiropractors

Net income for the chiropractic practice reached a high of over $101,000 in 1989, with gross income reaching its high in 1991 at over $234,000. Unfortunately, both figures have since fallen.

Impact of This Change

Chiropractors (indeed, all healthcare practitioners) can help stop this long-term slide in revenues by adding a nutrition system that will predictably run a nutrition profit center within their office. Since the multi-billion dollar nutrition industry can be used to support nearly all healthcare challenges, every practitioner should look at incorporating it into their practice. Adding a turnkey nutrition profit center to a practice must be an immediate consideration as a way to stop this downward trend and increase gross and net incomes.

3. Practice Overhead is Up for Chiropractors

The overhead for the average chiropractor has increased, so the percentage of net income derived out of gross income has gone down. For example, in 1980, chiropractors took home 52 percent of their gross income, but by 1997 that percentage had dropped below 38 percent.

Impact of This Change

Since 1980, chiropractors have been taking home less and less income every year. Chances are good that this is true for most other specialties as well. You must not only add a secondary nutrition profit center to increase your income, you also need to focus on reducing your practice overhead. When it comes to nutrition, one way to reduce overhead is to use Whole Body Alkaline Nutrition as opposed to the complicated, time-consuming Condition Specific approach. Condition Specific

Nutrition, as I've discussed before, requires an extensive inventory of products, ties up too much cash flow, requires additional staff, and wastes much of your clinical time. Whole Body Alkaline Nutrition, on the other hand, will increase income while reducing overhead by only requiring you to stock a limited number of nutrition products.

The Perfect Storm

Upon reviewing the three changes listed above, many chiropractors will see them adding up to the perfect storm of practice failure. Too many healthcare practitioners spend too much time worrying about changes like these and little-to-no time on how to make things better. Nutrition can provide one comprehensive solution. As I've said before, nutrition revenues are more than two and a half times larger than chiropractic revenues. We must embrace this and realize that the solution to ending the perfect storm lies within this fact.

The opportunity to take advantage of new and exciting options is the best part of change. See the move to nutrition as a great challenge and a chance to help more patients so that when you do move in that direction, the other negative practice changes will no longer be a threat.

Four Steps to Take Advantage of the Changing Landscape

1.) You must add a methodical and predictable Whole Body Alkaline Nutrition system to your practice as soon as possible as a secondary profit center to increase both gross and net incomes.

2.) You must create a marketing system or purchase a pre-designed turnkey system and implement it as soon as possible to increase new patient referrals, educate patients on the benefits of using nutrition along with your treatment program, and improve long-term relationships with existing patients.

3.) You must cut out all unnecessary practice expenses to lower your overhead. Focus on removing those things that serve very little purpose in terms of expanding the Equity of your practice, especially expensive Condition Specific Nutrition services.

4.) Equity is king! Move in the direction of building Equity in your practice. When the business world makes changes, embrace them and turn them into wins.

Don't let your practice run your life! We must tell our practice what we expect from it, or it will run rampant and abuse, use, and confuse us.

Do as Michael says, focus on the future and the most important form of money, the Equity in your practice. By taking control of your practice and implementing the changes I've suggested, you can feel confident again about reaching your practice goals with new energy and insight.

Is the picture beginning to formulate for you? We still have a few more topics before the puzzle is complete, so continue on to learn about Michael's advice on the subject of time. ✤

On the Subject of Time

Michael E. Gerber

Take time to deliberate; but when the time for action arrives, stop thinking and go in.

—Andrew Jackson

"I'm running out of time!" healthcare practitioners often lament. "I've got to learn how to manage my time more carefully!"

Of course, they see no real solution to this problem. They're just worrying the subject to death. Singing the healthcare practitioner's blues.

Some make a real effort to control time. Maybe they go to time management classes, or faithfully try to record their activities during every hour of the day.

But it's hopeless. Even when healthcare practitioners work harder, even when they keep precise records of their time, there's always a shortage of it. It's as if they're looking at a square clock in a round universe. Something doesn't fit. The result: the healthcare practitioner is constantly chasing work, money, life.

And the reason is simple. Healthcare practitioners don't see time for what it really is. They think of time with a small "t," rather than Time with a capital "T."

Yet Time is simply another word for *your life*. It's your ultimate asset, your gift at birth—and you can spend it any way you want. Do you know how you want to spend it? Do you have a plan?

How do *you* deal with Time? Are you even conscious of it? If you are, I bet you are constantly locked into either the future or the past. Relying on either memory or imagination.

Do you recognize these voices? "Once I get through this, I can have a drink . . . go on a vacation . . . retire." "I remember when I was young and practicing was satisfying."

As you go to bed at midnight, are you thinking about waking up at 7:00 a.m. so that you can get to the office by 8:00 a.m. so that you can go to lunch by noon, because your software people will be there at 1:30 p.m. and you've got a full schedule and a new patient scheduled for 2:30 p.m?

Most of us are prisoners of the future or the past. While pinballing between the two, we miss the richest moments of our life—the present. Trapped forever in memory or imagination, we are strangers to the here and now. Our future is nothing more than an extension of our past, and the present is merely the background.

It's sobering to think that right now each of us is at a precise spot somewhere between the beginning of our Time (our birth) and the end of our Time (our death). No wonder everyone frets about Time. What really terrifies us is that *we're using up our life and we can't stop it*.

It feels as if we're plummeting toward the end with nothing to break our free fall. Time is out of control! Understandably, this is horrifying, mostly because the real issue is not time with a small "t" but Death with a big "D."

From the depths of our existential anxiety, we try to put Time in a different perspective—all the while pretending we can manage it. We talk about Time as though it were something other than what it is. "Time is money," we announce, as though that explains it.

But what every healthcare practitioner should know is that Time is life. And Time ends! Life ends!

The big, walloping, irresolvable problem is that *we don't know how much Time we have left.*

Do you feel the fear? Do you want to get over it?

Let's look at Time more seriously.

To fully grasp Time with a capital "T," you have to ask the big Question: *How do I wish to spend the rest of my Time?*

Because I can assure you that if you don't ask that big Question with a big "Q," you will forever be assailed by the little questions. You'll shrink the whole of your life to *this time* and *next time* and the *last time*—all the while wondering, *what time is it?*

It's like running around the deck of a sinking ship worrying about where you left the keys to your cabin.

You must accept that you have only so much Time; that you're using up that Time second by precious second. And that your Time, your life, is the most valuable asset you have. Of course, you can use your Time any way you want. But unless you choose to use it as richly, as rewardingly, as excitingly, as intelligently, as *intentionally* as possible, you'll squander it and fail to appreciate it.

Indeed, if you are oblivious to the value of your Time, you'll commit the single greatest sin: You will live your life unconscious of its passing you by.

Until you deal with Time with a capital "T," you'll worry about time with a small "t" until you have no Time—or life—left. Then your Time will be history . . . along with your life.

I can anticipate the question: If Time is the problem, why not just take on fewer patients? Well, that's certainly an option, but probably not necessary. I know a chiropractor with a small practice who sees four times as many patients as the average, yet the doctor and staff don't work long hours. How is it possible?

This healthcare practitioner has a system. By using this expert system, the employees can do everything the healthcare practitioner or his associate healthcare practitioners would do—everything that isn't practitioner-dependent.

Be vs. Do

Remember when we all asked, "What do I want to be when I grow up?" It was one of our biggest concerns as children.

Notice that the question isn't, "What do I want to *do* when I grow up?" It's "What do I want to *be?*"

Shakespeare wrote, "To be or not to be." Not "To do or not to do."

But when you grow up, people always ask you, "What do you *do?*" How did the question change from *being* to *doing?* How did we miss the critical distinction between the two?

Even as children, we sensed the distinction. The real question we were asking was not what we would end up *doing* when we grew up, but who we would *be*.

We were talking about a *life* choice, not a *work* choice. We instinctively saw it as a matter of how we spend our Time, not what we do *in* time.

Look to children for guidance. I believe that as children we instinctively saw Time as life and tried to use it wisely. As children, we wanted to make a life choice, not a work choice. As children, we didn't know—or care—that work had to be done on time, on budget.

Until you see Time for what it really is—your life span—you will always ask the wrong question.

Until you embrace the whole of your Time and shape it accordingly, you will never be able to fully appreciate the moment.

Until you fully appreciate every second that comprises Time, you will never be sufficiently motivated to live those seconds fully.

Until you're sufficiently motivated to live those seconds fully, you will never see fit to change the way you are. You will never take the quality and sanctity of Time seriously.

And unless you take the sanctity of Time seriously, you will continue to struggle to catch up with something behind you. Your frustrations will mount as you try to snatch the second that just whisked by.

If you constantly fret about time with a small "t," then Time will blow right past you. And you'll miss the whole point, the real truth about Time: You can't manage it; you never could. You can only *live* it.

And so that leaves you with these questions: How do I live my life? How do I give significance to it? How can I be here now, in this moment?

Once you begin to ask these questions, you'll find yourself moving toward a much fuller, richer life. But if you continue to be caught up in the banal work you do every day, you're never going to find the time to take a deep breath, exhale, and be present in the now.

So, let's talk about the subject of *work*. But first, let's find out what Dr. Hayes has to say about time. ✤

Time is Your Life

Dr. Donald L. Hayes, DC

Time is the coin of your life. It is the only coin you have, and only you can determine how it will be spent. Be careful lest you let the other people spend it for you.

—Carl Sandburg

Michael's chapter on Time really hits home for me; he makes it perfectly clear that we can't manage time, we can only live it. So let's talk about that—how to live our time, the only time we have—the present. (For further reading on the subject of Time and living in the present, I highly recommend *The Power of Now* by Eckhart Tolle.) I'm going to work on this thing called Time and devise an efficient way for you to use yours more wisely when offering nutrition in your practice.

When I was consulting, I got to visit the offices of lots of the really big players who sold nutrition from their healthcare practices. I saw firsthand how much time it took these nutrition profit center giants to sell millions of dollars worth of supplements, and I was able to assess how they used their time. I must say that unless I met a very special doctor who had either found and implemented the E-Myth principles as I had done, or just had that certain time management business savvy mojo, most of them were completely out of control when it came to the time it took to operate their nutrition profit centers. I did the best I could to explain the E-Myth system and get them to understand that there was a better way of doing things, which would help them to "get a life."

Michael brings up a painful reality when he declares that "time" and "life" are basically the same thing, and therefore the time you have left is the life you have left. Once you stop and think about that, time becomes a whole different thing.

Most healthcare practitioners are very poor managers of time, and when they decide to add another clinical service like nutrition, most of them just manage to add another big time (read: life) waster.

If you want to add nutrition to your practice, you must do it in an efficient manner by using a healthcare practitioner system. If you attempt to use a more time-intensive model, one that requires setting time aside to schedule and conduct healthcare practitioner consultations, you'll quickly wonder why your life is passing you by.

A Time-Saving Approach to Nutrition

How do you implement nutrition so it won't be an added burden to your already busy practice schedule? The simplest way is to offer some type of nutrition that will support your efforts in managing a patient's main complaint. Patients are coming to you for help, typically to get relief from a current health challenge. You already know how to consult, examine, and determine a mode of treatment based on your primary healthcare training. So you have to incorporate nutrition into your existing treatment sequence.

This approach to nutrition should not be labor intensive for you, since the nutrition will be offered right alongside your other recommendations. It's vital that you do your due diligence, research your nutrition products thoroughly, and feel confident that the nutritional support package you're offering will, in fact, help improve a patient's outcome. When you have that certainty, the process will be very efficient.

It's imperative that you detach yourself from the patient's decision to accept both your regular treatment and the nutrition. It's not about convincing the patient to take the nutrition products you offer; it's about offering a nutrition package that you know will help improve healing time and overall outcome if the patient chooses it, but you always respect their decision.

Of course, if any patient has questions about why they need the nutrition, and you have the time, do the best you can to help. If you don't have the time, have a key staff person take it a step further, but under no condition should you try and "sell" the products—that's not the way to make nutrition work.

The Notorious Time Log

I know you don't want to hear this, but I must suggest that, to prepare for adding a nutrition profit center to your practice, you should conduct a time log on your current clinical services.

After all, one of the keys to managing your time better is to find out how you are currently spending it. This project should take no more than a few days. At the conclusion of the process you will immediately acquire some valuable insight into how you can better manage your clinical time and see for yourself how best to fit nutrition into your practice.

What we're looking for from this exercise is how you, the doctor, are currently spending your time. Therefore, it's an absolute must that you record the time you start and stop all activities that involve you.

A stopwatch is very helpful in determining the exact amount of time you spend on various procedures. Try to be as accurate as possible and once you have the raw data, sort it into specific categories:

consultations, examinations, treatments, reports of findings, phone calls, emails, administrative tasks, working with staff, and so on.

Calculate the percentage of time that is being spent by you on each activity. If you're like most healthcare practitioners, you'll find some key time wasters like phone calls, emails, and surfing the web. It's up to you to evaluate each task and stop those that are unproductive and keeping you from completing the important tasks. I suggest that when you're at work, spend your time doing the things only a doctor can do, and save the time wasters for your off-duty hours.

Here are a few other suggestions that will help you become more efficient and have more time to balance your regular clinical services so you can easily fit nutrition into the practice mix:

Use systems. As I have said before, there are only two ways to get things done in your practice that need to get done, but aren't getting done: either create or purchase a system that will handle the task. When you determine what a clinical hour of your time is worth in terms of practice revenue, you'll quickly realize that anything you're doing that could be completed within a system is bound to be less than your hourly rate.

Make sure your staff is not wasting your time. Many times, staff will try to impress you by taking up too much office time asking questions they already know the answers to. By conducting regular staff meetings on how all of you can best use your clinical time, you'll be able to establish a very efficient work schedule for everyone.

Have your staff conduct a time log as well. Most offices find that staff have time wasters in their day as well, and there are quite a few hours that could be put to more productive use.

If you find that you're wasting time, don't just take on fewer patients; create and use a system that enables staff to do everything that isn't dependent on your expertise as a healthcare practitioner. Remember, you can offer nutrition effectively and add time to your patients' lives while getting more time for your own life in the bargain.

Now, it seems, is the perfect time to introduce a new concept: one having to do with Michael's ideas on work. ❦

On the Subject
of Work

Michael E. Gerber

*The man who has the largest capacity for work and thought is the man
who is bound to succeed.*

—Henry Ford

I n the business world, as the saying goes, the entrepreneur
knows something about everything, the technician knows everything about something, and the switchboard operator just
knows everything.

In a practice, healthcare practitioners see their natural work
as the work of the technician. The Supreme Technician. Often to
the exclusion of everything else.

After all, healthcare practitioners get zero preparation working
as a manager and spend no time thinking as an entrepreneur—
those just aren't courses offered in today's schools and colleges. By
the time they own their own practice, they're just doing it, doing
it, doing it.

At the same time, they want everything—freedom, respect, money. Most of all, they want to rid themselves of meddling bosses and start their own practice. That way they can be their own boss and take home all the money. These healthcare practitioners are in the throes of an entrepreneurial seizure.

Healthcare practitioners who have been praised for their ability to treat difficult cases or their extensive knowledge of natural health-care sciences believe they have what it takes to run a practice. It's not unlike the plumber who becomes a contractor because he's a great plumber. Sure, he may be a great plumber . . . but it doesn't necessarily follow that he knows how to build a practice that does this work.

It's the same for a healthcare practitioner. So many of them are surprised to wake up one morning and discover that they're nowhere near as equipped for owning their own practice as they thought they were.

More than any other subject, work is the cause of obsessive-compulsive behavior by healthcare practitioners.

Work. You've got to do it every single day.

Work. If you fall behind, you'll pay for it.

Work. There's either too much or not enough.

So many healthcare practitioners describe work as what they do when they're busy. Some discriminate between the work they *could* be doing as healthcare practitioners and the work they *should* be doing as healthcare practitioners.

But according to the E-Myth, they're exactly the same thing. The work you *could* do and the work you *should* do as a practitioner are identical. Let me explain.

Strategic Work vs. Tactical Work

Healthcare practitioners can do only two kinds of work: strategic work and tactical work.

Tactical work is easier to understand, because it's what almost every practitioner does almost every minute of every hour of every day. It's called getting the job done. It's called doing business.

Tactical work includes filing, billing, answering the telephone, going to the bank, and seeing patients.

The E-Myth says that tactical work is all the work healthcare practitioners find themselves doing in a healthcare practice to *avoid* doing the strategic work.

"I'm too busy," most practitioners will tell you.

"How come nothing goes right unless I do it myself?" they complain in frustration.

Practitioners say these things when they're up to their ears in tactical work. But most practitioners don't understand that if they had done more strategic work, they would have less tactical work to do.

Healthcare practitioners are doing strategic work when they ask the following questions:

- Why am I a healthcare practitioner?
- What will my practice look like when it's done?
- What must my practice look, act, and feel like in order for it to compete successfully?
- What are the key indicators of my practice?

Please note that I said healthcare practitioners *ask* these questions when they are doing strategic work. I didn't say these are the questions they necessarily answer.

That is the fundamental difference between strategic work and tactical work. Tactical work is all about *answers*: How to do this. How to do that.

Strategic work, in contrast, is all about *questions*: What practice are we really in? Why are we in that practice? Who specifically is our practice determined to serve? When will I sell this practice? How and where will this practice be doing business when I sell it? And so forth.

Not that strategic questions don't have answers. healthcare practitioners who commonly ask strategic questions know that once they ask such a question, they're already on their way to *envisioning* the answer. Question and answer are part of a whole. You can't find the right answer until you've asked the right question.

Tactical work is much easier, because the question is always more obvious. In fact, you don't ask the tactical question; instead, the question arises from a result you need to get or a problem you need to solve. Billing a patient is tactical work. Evaluating a patient is tactical work. Firing an employee is tactical work. Recommending a nutritional supplement is tactical work.

Tactical work is the stuff you do every day in your practice. Strategic work is the stuff you plan to do to create an exceptional practice/business/enterprise.

In tactical work, the question comes from *out there* rather than *in here*. The tactical question is about something *outside* of you, whereas the strategic question is about something *inside* of you.

The tactical question is about something you *need* to do, whereas the strategic question is about something you *want* to do. Want versus need.

If tactical work consumes you,

- you are always reacting to something outside of you;
- your practice runs you, you don't run it;
- your employees run you, you don't run them; and
- your life runs you, you don't run your life.

You must understand that the more strategic work you do, the more intentional your decisions, your practice, and your life become. *Intention* is the byword of strategic work.

Everything on the outside begins to serve you, to serve your vision, rather than forcing you to serve it. Everything you *need* to do is congruent with what you *want* to do. It means you have a vision, an aim, a purpose, a strategy, an *envisioned* result.

Strategic work is the work you do to *design* your practice, to design your life.

Tactical work is the work you do to *implement* the design created by strategic work.

Without strategic work, there is no design. Without strategic work, all that's left is keeping busy.

There's only one thing left to do. It's time to take action. But first, let's see what Dr. Hayes has to say on the subject of work. ❧

Work Smarter, Not Harder

Dr. Donald L. Hayes, DC

Without ambition one starts nothing. Without work one finishes nothing.
The prize will not be sent to you. You have to earn it.

—Ralph Waldo Emerson

Now that Michael has illuminated the fact that there are only two kinds of work—strategic and tactical—it's time to apply them to setting up a nutrition system that will run your nutrition profit center, one that you can easily integrate into your life.

I know you probably haven't had any training whatsoever on how to design and market a nutrition profit center, or how to use nutrition as a primary lead generator to attract new patients. It's safe to say that those two skills might just be on the bottom of your "ability-to-do" list.

Never fear! I'm going to share with you the strategic and tactical work that is required to design and operate a nutrition system that will run your nutrition profit center.

The Strategic and Tactical Work of a Nutrition Profit Center

It is imperative that you spend a considerable amount of quality time designing the system that will run your nutrition profit center day in and day out. Creating a system that everyone in your office can easily follow is the strategic work of your nutrition profit center.

The tactical work of a nutrition profit center is the easy part. All that is required is that you and your team follow the system you have created to the letter, each and every day.

A 3-Step Whole Body Alkaline Nutrition System

Let me share with you a 3-Step Whole Body Alkaline Nutrition System that can improve the lives of everyone you recommend it to and, in turn, make your nutrition profit center very successful. This nutrition system is steeped in science and founded on solid research, and provides the most good for the most patients while requiring the least amount of clinical time from both healthcare practitioner and staff. The majority of patient outcomes will be improved using the three steps in this system as recommended, leaving only a small portion of individuals who may require an additional targeted nutritional supplement.

Whole Body Alkaline Nutrition in 3 Steps:

Step 1. Raise Internal pH and Alkalize the Body

The abbreviation pH stands for "potential of hydrogen." The pH of a fluid tells you how acid or alkaline it is. pH is measured on a scale from 0-14 and 7.0 is neutral. Anything less than 7.0 is acidic and anything greater than 7.0 is alkaline. The blood must maintain a pH level between 7.35 and 7.45. Less oxygen is present when pH is below 7.0, which is why all pathogens thrive in an acidic environment. An acidic condition is a breeding ground for unhealthy bacteria, yeast, and fungi that may contribute to pain and inflammation. When your diet and lifestyle become too acidic, you create fertile ground for pathogens to multiply and flourish. But they can't survive with alkalinity, which is why raising internal pH is so central to a healthy lifestyle.

Research on Helping the Body Stay pH Balanced

Since the early 1930s, scientists and leading healthcare practitioners have recognized that in order for the body to remain vital, energetic, and healthy, the general pH of the human system (also referred to as the acid/alkaline balance) must remain alkaline. The body continually strives on a daily basis to maintain an alkaline environment, and when that balance is compromised, many health problems may occur.

It is widely accepted and well documented that internal pH plays a critical role in the healthy function of various types of tissues and organs. It is also recognized that a more alkaline environment is generally healthier than an acidic one, except in the stomach where more acidic conditions provide stronger protection against pathogens entering the digestive system.

The pH value is highly controlled in all biological fluids and tissues. Moreover, each cell, tissue, or organ type—such as the stomach, muscles, or blood—has its own optimal pH level (1). Blood pH is strictly regulated within its physiological boundaries. Several natural "buffer systems" in the human body contribute to this homeostasis, which is maintained via metabolic and respiratory pathways mainly in the kidneys, lungs and other tissues.

More importantly, it has been reported that acidification of bio-fluids in the human body may result in a number of detrimental effects. Several studies have shown that acidic pH increases expression and production of pro-inflammatory interleukin 6 and 8. They have also indicated that this induction is due to activation of Nf-KB, a master gene involved in controlling inflammation (2,3). Other studies have shown that alkaline pH in the body significantly improves antioxidant potency of natural products (4-6). These studies also indicated that acidic body conditions may significantly reduce the antioxidant potency of ingested fruits and vegetables. Other significant pathological aspects of acidic pH were reported by scientists working with infectious bacteria. As reported, acidic pH strongly contributes to pathologies related to infection by Candida albicans. It is also important to mention that under acidic conditions, glucose and fat metabolism are unfavorably influenced.

Most People Over Forty Are Acidic

Today, many patients have a diet and lifestyle that is extremely acidic. The foods they eat on a regular basis—such as pasteurized dairy products, meats, trans fats, cooked oils, baked goods, refined sugars, coffee and carbonated drinks—are all acid-forming. Stress, pharmaceutical drugs, alcohol, and stimulants are additional factors that lead to an acid buildup in their bodies.

Research conducted at the University of San Francisco Department of Medicine by Drs. Lynda Frassetto and Anthony Sebastian, and published in the prestigious *Journal of Gerontology*, clearly demonstrates that as we get older, our bodies accumulate acid wastes. These scientists reported a significant increase in blood acidity and a correspondingly significant loss of alkaline reserves with increasing age from twenty to ninety years, indicative of a progressively worsening low-level metabolic acidosis.

The research clearly shows that the alkaline reserves of humans remain fairly constant until the age of forty when they begin to decrease severely. Coincidentally, the researchers noted that adult degenerative diseases such as obesity, diabetes, heart disease, osteoporosis, high blood pressure and others start to appear at the age of forty and gradually worsen with age. The researchers attribute the accumulation of acid and the reduction of the alkaline state as we age to eating the Standard American Diet and conclude that the role of age-related metabolic acidosis as a cause of adult degenerative disease warrants consideration (7).

Where Does the Acid Go?

When you have too much acid in your body, it first goes to the kidneys for elimination. When the kidneys are at full capacity and they can't accept all the acid that is being produced, the body directs the acid toward the alkaline minerals in your system, which act as buffers and mix with the acids so they eventually become neutral salts. However, if you don't have enough alkaline minerals in reserve, the body is forced to borrow minerals, including calcium, sodium, potassium and magnesium, from vital organs and bones to neutralize the acid and safely remove it from the body. Because of the stress of this high acidity, the body can suffer severe and prolonged damage, a condition that may go undetected for years.

Measure pH and Inflammation Levels with Saliva Testing

Research on Diabetology and Metabolic Syndrome entitled "Saliva pH as a Marker of Adiponectin Levels in Women" (published by the Department of Medicine at the University of Montreal in conjunction with the Canadian Institutes of Health Research in January 2012) clearly shows that testing saliva with pH paper is an inexpensive, non-invasive way to measure acid-alkaline balance and levels of inflammation.

The study explained that saliva pH has a direct, linear correlation to adiponectin, an anti-inflammatory blood serum hormone. The research showed that as saliva pH gets more acidic, blood adiponectin levels decrease and cardiometabolic risk components such as inflammation, oxidative stress, dyslipidemia, type-2 diabetes, hypertension, and cardiovascular disease all increase. The scientists concluded: "Saliva pH may allow a better monitoring of the health status and disease onset than traditional blood sampling" (8).

The Best Way to Help the Body Stay pH Balanced

Current studies provide clinical evidence that consuming a blend of natural vegetable and fruit ingredients will increase the pH value in the human body. Research results indicate that ingestion of as little as three grams of a high quality fruit and vegetable powdered supplement at bedtime resulted in an increased pH value in urine collected the following morning. On average, the pH value increased by 0.5 pH units following a single dose. The pH scale is logarithmic, so a 0.5 pH value shift from say, 6.5 pH to 7.0 pH, would mean that the new value is five times more alkaline. This is a very significant clinical improvement from just one serving! Based on these research results, it's easy to understand why frequent use of this type of supplement may result in maintenance of a healthy pH level in the human body.

Step 2. Reduce Inflammation and Quench All Five Types of Free Radicals

Regardless of your specialty, your patients are coming to you on their first visit with a main complaint that includes some degree of inflammation.

There are two distinct types of inflammation. The first is acute inflammation, which results in acute pain. This is considered classical inflammation. The second type is chronic low-level inflammation that is often below the threshold of pain until it gets triggered by some event, at which point it becomes symptomatic.

Accidents, injuries and illnesses are part of the fabric of life, and healing those conditions is the body's self-repair process. All healing begins with inflammation, which is the body's natural attempt to repair damaged tissue. So if inflammation is natural, why does it underlie almost every serious health issue facing modern society? The answer begins with free radicals.

Free radicals are reactive species that can have adverse effects on normal physiological functions. Studies associate the five major types of free radicals with chronic inflammation and other health conditions. Reactive Oxygen Species (ROS) and Reactive Nitrogen Species (RNS) are terms that collectively describe free radicals. Free radicals are formed when the chemical bonds of a molecule are broken, leaving one or more unpaired electrons in the outer shell. These unpaired electrons harmfully react with various substrates in the body such as lipids, proteins, and DNA. Free radicals contribute to "oxidative stress" and "nitrosative stress," processes that have been linked to numerous diseases and degenerative health conditions such as chronic inflammation, cardiovascular disease, hypertension, carcinogenesis, Alzheimer's disease, Parkinson's disease, diabetes, aging, DNA damage, and certain cancers.

The Five Major Types of Free Radicals

There are five major types of free radicals of concern to humans:

1. **Hydroxyl Radicals** are the most reactive of the ROS and incapable of elimination by the body's endogenous enzymes. Hydroxyl radicals attack almost all types of macromolecules, including carbohydrates, nucleic acids, lipids, and amino acids. Hydroxyl radicals are linked to DNA damage and cancer.

2. **Peroxyl Radicals** target lipids in order to take their electrons, thereby damaging the cells. Highly unstable and readily reactive to molecular oxygen, Peroxyl radicals are associated with cardiovascular diseases and atherosclerosis.

3. **Peroxynitrite Radicals** are created by a reaction between nitric oxide and superoxide and contribute to the

breakdown of vital proteins such as collagen and exert strong oxidizing properties on many cellular constituents including sulfydryls, lipids, amino acids, and nucleotides. Excess peroxynitrite formation may be involved in the development of certain cancers, hepatitis, chronic inflammation, and neurodegenerative conditions such as Alzheimer's and Parkinson's diseases.

4. **Singlet Oxygen Radicals,** highly unstable and durable, are generated in the skin by UV exposure and are linked to eye diseases like macular degeneration, as well as cholesterol problems and cardiovascular diseases.

5. **Superoxide Anions** are highly toxic free radicals that contribute to lipid and DNA damage, and are associated with hypertension, cardiovascular damage, and mitochondrial diseases.

The Next Generation of Quenching Free Radicals

When most healthcare practitioners consider inflammation clinically, they tend to focus their attention on the pain, swelling, heat, and redness that typically follow an accident or acute injury and are a result of the body's normal inflammatory response to cellular destruction.

Current pathology textbooks teach that the inflammatory process is a complex interaction that involves both pro- and anti-inflammatory phases. The pro-inflammatory phase lets the body know that tissue damage is occurring and stimulates the healing process. The anti-inflammatory mechanism of the process can then begin cellular repair and regeneration. Only when these two phases are continually balanced can the body effectively repair the damaged tissues.

Even though chronic inflammation is a component of virtually all known diseases, it remains a symptom rather than the basic cause of these diseases. When you study the science, you'll see that chronic inflammation is the consequence of some type of trigger, such as an injury to the body, combined with an acid-alkaline pH imbalance and micronutrient deficiency. When trying to properly support the body's attempt to reduce chronic inflammation, the nutritional component is essential because it helps correct the underlying abnormal acidic body fluid pH levels and provides a full-spectrum antioxidant designed to act on and neutralize each of the five distinct types of free radicals.

Antioxidant Activity on Free Radicals

Antioxidants function as a vital line of defense against free radicals by quenching their appetite for DNA, vital proteins, lipids, and amino acids. By scavenging free radicals, antioxidants help prevent oxidative and nitrosative stress. Because the body's systems for eliminating free radicals are not 100 percent effective, supplementing the diet with food and functional food products rich in antioxidants is vital to controlling the damage caused by free radicals.

A superior quality, highly concentrated antioxidant supplement that is made from fruit, vegetable, and herb extract ingredients will provide the most benefit. The supplement should contain all five distinct phytochemical formulations that act on each of the five major types of free radicals:

1. **HORAC Formulation:** The hydroxyl-targeting antioxidants come from phytochemicals found in turmeric, garlic, basil, oregano, and cinnamon.

2. **ORAC Formulation:** The peroxyl-targeting antioxidants come from phytochemicals found in broccoli sprout, onion, tomato, carrot, spinach, kale and brussel sprouts.

3. **NORAC Formulation:** The peroxynitrite-targeting antioxidants come from phytochemicals found in acerola, camu camu, quercetin, acai and mangosteen.

4. **SOAC Formulation:** The singlet-oxygen targeting antioxidants come from phytochemicals found in blackcurrant, blueberry, sweet cherry, acai, blackberry, chokeberry, raspberry, and bilberry.

5. **SORAC Formulation:** The superoxide anion-targeting antioxidants come from phytochemicals found in apple, elderberry and blue corn.

Inflammation does not result from a deficiency of aspirin, cortisone, or any other anti-inflammatory drug. Rather, the research supports a desperate need for healthcare practitioners to use antioxidant rich, Whole Body Alkaline Nutrition to help improve the body's state of alkalization and satisfy its basic need for nutrients that deliver five-dimensional free radical quenching. No drug can ever make up for a nutritional deficiency. When patients come to you suffering from some underlying form of inflammation, be it acute or chronic, it is vital that you nourish their biochemistry with the best form of Whole Body Alkaline Nutrition.

The Pathology of Inflammation

The premier pathology textbook used by the majority of healthcare practitioners in school today is *The Pathologic Basis of Disease* by Robbins and Cotran. The textbook consists of twenty-nine chapters with the first three chapters dedicated to the explanation of acute and chronic inflammation and the remaining twenty-six chapters focused on all known pathological diseases. The aim of the first three chapters is to inform doctors that nearly all of the diseases they will experience from patients while in private practice are due in large part to, and will have a significant component of, systemic inflammation and free radical damage. As a healthcare practitioner practicing today, it is incumbent on you to help patients deal with both acute and chronic inflammation.

Mom was Right—Fruits and Vegetables Do It All

What's the most researched and documented way to reduce inflammation, improve pH, neutralize free radicals, and alkalize the body? Eat more fruits and vegetables! A quick Google search on "research supporting eating fruits and vegetables" listed over a million supporting documents, including the USDA's website. The research on the anti-inflammatory benefits of eating fruits and vegetables is overwhelming; here are just two of the endless published scientific research articles for your review.

Journal of the American Dietetic Association

The first study, entitled "Fruit and Vegetable Consumption and its Relation to Markers of Inflammation and Oxidative Stress in Adolescents," was published in the *Journal of the American Dietetic Association*. By way of background, the study stated that fruits and vegetables, rich in flavonoids and antioxidants, have been associated with lower risk of stroke and coronary heart disease, and a decreased prevalence of markers of inflammation and oxidative stress in adults.

Markers of inflammation and oxidative stress are predictors of coronary heart disease risk; however, it was unknown whether these markers related to dietary flavonoid and antioxidant intake in youth. The research sought to determine whether greater intake of fruits and vegetables, antioxidants, and flavonoids was inversely associated with markers of inflammation and oxidative stress in 285 adolescent boys and girls aged thirteen to seventeen years. In their conclusion, the researchers stated that the results show that the beneficial effects of fruit and vegetable intake on markers of inflammation and oxidative stress are already present by early adolescence and provide support for the Dietary Guidelines for Americans "to consume five or more servings per day" of fruits and vegetables to promote beneficial cardiovascular health (9).

American Journal of Clinical Nutrition

The second study, entitled "Fruit and Vegetable Intakes, C-Reactive Protein, and the Metabolic Syndrome," was published in the *American Journal of Clinical Nutrition*. The objective of the study was to evaluate the relationship between fruit and vegetable intake and C-Reactive Protein (CRP) concentration, a major inflammatory marker of the prevalence of the metabolic syndrome. In the conclusion of the study, the researchers reported that higher intakes of fruits and vegetables were associated with a lower risk of the metabolic syndrome and that the lower risk may be the result of lower CRP concentrations. The scientists went on to say that their findings support current dietary recommendations to increase daily intakes of fruit and vegetables as a primary preventive measure against cardiovascular disease (10).

How To Decrease C-Reactive Protein

CRP is an immune recognition protein that is a sensitive marker of inflammation, commonly used as a diagnostic for the presence of acute or chronic health problems. Elevated circulating levels of CRP have been associated with a wide range of inflammation-related conditions such as diabetes, cardiovascular disease, osteoarthritis, osteoporosis, and increased risk of fractures. Basically, a reduction in levels of CRP indicates a reduction of inflammation.

Calcium Fructoborate (CF) is a mineral complex found in fruits, vegetables, legumes, and herbs, that has been the subject of over a dozen published studies on its unique properties and potential health benefits, especially for conditions linked to inflammation such as bone, joint, and cardiovascular conditions. Recently published human clinical research has demonstrated CF's ability to modulate key markers associated with inflammation-related conditions such as osteoarthritis (11,12) and angina pectoris (13), and has included accompanying subjective reports of improvement in feelings of pain, as well as increased comfort and quality of life (11-13). In particular, the studies indicate that CF significantly reduces elevated serum levels of CRP in humans.

Results of Clinical Studies on Calcium Fructoborate

- Study #1: Double-blind, placebo-controlled study on healthy subjects, ten subjects per group. CF supplementation tested over a fourteen-day period at a serving of 108 mg twice per day. CRP was reduced by 37% versus baseline, pre-supplementation value. CF also induced a 19% increase in endogenous levels of calcitriol, the active form of Vitamin D3 (11).

- Study #2: Double-blind, placebo-controlled study on health subjects, fifteen subjects per group. CF supplementation tested over a fourteen day period at a serving of 28.5 mg twice per day. CRP was reduced by 60.25% versus baseline, pre-supplementation value. The CF group also experienced a reduction in elevated levels of erythrocyte sedimentation rate (-10.25%) and fibrinogen (-13.73%), two other common measures of inflammation (12).

- Study #3: Double-blind, active-controlled (existing treatment protocol) study on subjects with stable angina pectoris, twenty-nine subjects per group. CF supplementation tested over a sixty day period at a serving of 112 mg once per day. CRP was reduced by 39.7% versus baseline, pre-supplementation value. The CF group also experienced a 5.9% reduction in total cholesterol, a 9.2% reduction in LDL cholesterol, a 5.1% increase in HDL cholesterol, and a 48.8% reduction in angina episodes per week (13).

Together, these results provide strong evidence for Calcium Fructoborate's ability to improve inflammatory status in human subjects. This plant-based mineral complex stands out as a compelling, proven powdered ingredient that should be included in nutrition products designed to support healthy inflammation management, cardiovascular health, and bone health.

Fruit and Vegetable Powders Are as Good as Real Produce

The British Journal of Nutrition reported their findings in a published article entitled, "Changes in plasma antioxidant status following consumption of diets high or low in fruit and vegetables or following dietary supplementation with an antioxidant mixture." The study concluded that low temperature air-dried fruit and vegetable powdered supplements did, in fact, significantly increase the plasma antioxidant concentrations by the same measure as did real produce (14).

Step 3. Promote Healthy Weight Management

It has been estimated that two billion people worldwide suffer from at least one form of micronutrient deficiency. Sub-optimal intake of certain micronutrients is scientifically linked to chronic inflammation and other dangerous and debilitating diseases such as cardiovascular disease, osteoporosis, cancer, resistance to infection, and birth defects. Several scientific studies have established a strong correlation between micronutrient deficiency and the condition of overweight/obesity, including one study that found that the likelihood of being overweight or obese increased significantly in micronutrient deficient subjects (15).

Journal of the International Society of Sports Nutrition

With more than two-thirds of the U.S. population overweight or obese, and research showing that one-third of Americans are on a diet at any given time, a research study published in the *Journal of the International Society of Sports Nutrition* in 2010 set out to determine if four of the most popular whole food diet plans could protect followers from micronutrient deficiency.

The research study had no human participants, but instead analyzed the sufficiency level of 27 essential micronutrients, as determined by the U.S. Food and Drug Administration (FDA) Reference Daily Intake (RDI) guidelines.

Four popular whole food based diet plans were selected for study that included, (1) "Atkins For Life," a low-carbohydrate diet; (2) "The South Beach Diet," a medically based modified low-carbohydrate diet recommended by a wide variety of medical and governmental organizations; (3) "The DASH Diet" (Dietary Approaches to Stop Hypertension), an eating plan promoted by the National Heart, Lung, and Blood Institute; and (4) "The Best Life Diet," by Bob Greene (Oprah Winfrey's weight loss expert) that emphasizes swapping unhealthy foods for healthier ones.

The research found that all four diet plans failed to deliver 100 percent sufficiency for the selected 27 essential micronutrients when followed as recommended by their suggested daily menus. The question of whether an individual can obtain RDI sufficiency of twenty-seven essential micronutrients from a balanced, whole food diet alone was answered in this study as it relates to the four selected popular diet plans (16).

These selected diet plans are presented to the public as sound, healthy, balanced diets. They recommend their followers eat a variety of fresh fruits and vegetables, whole grains, and lean proteins, and yet, not one of the whole food eating plans was able to provide RDI sufficiency of the twenty-seven essential micronutrients selected for the study.

The study concluded that anyone following one of the selected four eating plans, or any similar ones using whole foods, would be, on average, deficient in 56 percent or fifteen out of twenty-seven of the selected essential micronutrients, based on the FDA's RDI guidelines.

The implications of this study are significant and far-reaching, showing that an individual following a popular diet plan using food alone has a high likelihood of becoming micronutrient deficient, a condition that has been shown to cause an 80.8 percent increase in the likelihood of becoming overweight or obese and is scientifically linked to a host of chronic diseases (16).

Based on the results of this research and other similarly conclusive studies, the belief that a healthy, balanced diet can consistently deliver all of the essential vitamins and minerals through whole food alone is in need of revision. Clearly, supplementation should be considered as a viable, low-cost method to achieve micronutrient sufficiency and reduce the risk for some of today's most prevalent and devastating health conditions and diseases (16-18).

A Whole Body Alkaline Nutrition Shake is the Solution to Micronutrient Deficiency

If you don't have a nutrition supplement recommendation that combines protection from micronutrient deficiency with healthy weight management, you are doing your patients a huge disservice. In addition to the research above, a recent health report predicted that obesity-related illness will raise national health care costs by $48 billion annually over the next two decades by adding another 7.9 million new cases of diabetes, 5 million cases of chronic heart disease and stroke, and 400,000 cancer cases. How can any health-care practitioner ignore these frightening forecasts?

The best way to combat these dire statistics is to recommend a full-spectrum, nutrient dense, nutritionally balanced meal replacement that can also help raise internal pH, decrease inflammation, neutralize all five types of free radicals, alkalize the body, and assist in weight management.

This type of Whole Body Alkaline Nutrition shake is actually a meal that can help curb cravings for sugar and junk food. The product should not only promote weight loss, but also help to increase energy levels, improve digestion and regularity, and support the immune system by providing 100 percent whole food goodness from several different nutrient groups. It should contain plant-based proteins and essential amino acids from sources like brown rice, pea, flaxseed, chia, sacha inchi, amaranth and quinoa. It should also include plant-based essential healthy oils, phytonutrients, antioxidants, probiotics and prebiotics, adaptogenic herbs, digestive enzymes, and vitamins, and minerals.

The product should be an all-in-one blend of all three food groups that helps the body eliminate toxins that tend to build up in the digestive tract over the years due to eating the Standard American Diet (SAD). A healthy digestive tract supports the body's ability to absorb the nutrients a person needs in order to lose weight and maintain health and vitality.

During the process of the body cleansing itself from the inside out, whole food ingredients deliver the essential nutrients the body needs to help curb its cravings. The body stores acid from sugary, processed junk foods in fat cells in order to keep the acid poisons out of the blood stream and vital organs. When you help your patients nourish their body at the cellular level, their body will begin to balance and they will start to shed excess fat. When pH balance is achieved, the body instinctively strives to drop to its ideal, healthy weight.

To lose weight, a patient can simply substitute two of their three daily whole food meals with a high-quality meal replacement shake. As the body begins to shed stored fat, the super foods, antioxidants, and phytonutrients will continue to help support the normal inflammatory response and maintain proper acid-alkaline balance which will, in turn, help facilitate ongoing proper muscle function and connective tissue repair.

To maintain weight and maximize health, a patient can substitute one meal replacement shake for one of their daily meals. To gain weight, the patient adds three meal replacement shakes to their regular three meals per day. Patients should also follow prudent lifestyle guidelines for diet, exercise, and stress reduction.

How to Market a Nutrition Profit Center

The strategic and tactical work of marketing a nutrition profit center and generating a steady flow of new patients is an area where few, if any, healthcare practitioners are prepared or qualified to do. Unfortunately, many doctors either think they have this skill, but do it poorly, or feel it's not important, so they don't attempt to market their nutrition profit center at all. Either assumption can result in a huge financial disaster because of the lost opportunity to build a very profitable ongoing nutrition profit center.

Due to the tremendous competition within healthcare, most hospitals and large medical groups today pay a considerable amount of money to marketing firms to help promote their business and attract a steady stream of new patients. Individual healthcare practitioners don't have the deep pockets that the larger medical institutions have, and since they don't possess the skill set they need to market themselves, most of their practices fail to grow!

Therefore, individual doctors need to recognize that when it comes to the strategic and tactical work of marketing their nutrition profit center and generating new patients, they will best be served by using some type of turnkey, fully-automated system that is inexpensive, yet highly effective at stimulating referrals, educating existing patients on nutrition, and increasing monthly nutrition sales.

Delegating a major portion of marketing your nutrition profit center and attracting new patients to a proven turnkey no inventory online nutrition store, as detailed in Chapter 18, requires little to no time from you or your staff, and can become a tremendous income generator for your practice.

You must do your due diligence and make sure that the nutrition company and the online nutrition store you choose to represent your practice is of the highest quality. Poor marketing is no better than no marketing; in fact, it might even be worse.

Are you ready to offer nutrition in your practice, help a lot of patients, and tap into the unlimited financial potential in nutrition today? Then you must incorporate a nutrition system to run your nutrition profit center and add a hands-free online nutrition store so your patients and other customers can purchase nutrition products directly from you.

That's the work that must be done, and the surest way to nutrition profit center success.

Now all the pieces are in place—the only thing left to do is take action. Let's turn to Michael, now, for his thoughts on how to take the knowledge you've gained and put it to use. ✤

REFERENCES:

1. Richard A. Calderone and Ronald L Cihlar, "Fungal Pathogenesis: Principles and Clinical Applications," *Mycology* 14 (2002): 140-152.

2. Lei Xu and Isaiah J. Fidler, "Acidic-pH-Induced Elevation in Interleukin-8 Expression by Human Ovarian Carcinoma Cells," *Cancer Research* 60 (200): 4610-4616.

3. Parvaneh Rafiee, Victoria M. Nelson, Sharon Manley, Michael Wellner, Martin Floer, David G. Binion, Reza Shaker, "Effect of Curcumin on Acidic-pH-Induced Expression of IL-6 and IL-8 in Human Esophageal Epithelial Cells (HET-1A): Role of PKC, MAPKs, and NF-kB," *American Journal of Physiology - Gastrointestinal and Liver Physiology* 296 (2009): G388-G398.

4. Tomasz Borkowski, Henryk Szymusiak, Anna Gliszczynska-Swiglo, Ivonne M. C. M. Rietjens, and Bozena Tyrakowska, "Radical Scavenging Capacity of Wine Anthocyanins is Strongly pH-Dependent," *Journal of Agricultural and Food Chemistry* 53(14) (2005): 5526-34, doi:10.1021/jf0478556.

5. Katarzyna Lemanska, Henryk Szymusiak, Bozena Tyrakowska, Ryszard Zielinski, Ans E.M.F Soffers, and Ivonne M. C. M. Rietjens, "The Influence of pH on Antioxidant Properties and the Mechanism of Antioxidant Action of Hydroxyflavones," *Free Radical Biology and Medicine* 31(7) (2001): 869-81.

6. Anna Gliszczynska-Swiglo, Henryk Szymusiak, and Paulina Malinowska, "Betanin, The Main Pigment of Red Beet: Molecular Origin of its Exceptionally High Free Radical-Scavenging Activity," *Food Additives and Contaminants* 23(11) (2006): 1079-87, doi:10.1080/02652030600986032.

7. Lynda Frassetto and Anthony Sebastian, "Age and Systemic Acid-Base Equilibrium: Analysis of Published Data," *Journal of Gerontology: Biological Sciences* 51A(1) (1996): B91-99, doi:10.1093/gerona/51A.1.B91.

8. Monique Tremblay, Yacine Loucif, Julie Methot, Diane Brisson and Daniel Gaudet, "Salivary pH as a Marker of Plasma Adiponectin Concentrations in Women," *Diabetology and Metabolic Syndrome* 4(4) (2012), doi:10.1186/1758-5996-4-4

9. Erica M. Holt, Lyn M. Steffen, Antoinette Moran, Samar Basu, Julia Steinberger, Julie A. Ross, Ching-Ping Hong, and Alan R. Sinaiko, "Fruit and Vegetable Consumption and its Relation to Markers of Inflammation and Oxidative Stress in Adolescents," *Journal of the Academy of Nutrition and Dietetics*, 109(3) (2009): 414-421.

10. Ahmad Esmaillzadeh, Masoud Kimiagar, Yadollah Mehrabi, Leila Azadbakht, Frank B. Hu, and Walter C. Willett, "Fruit and Vegetable Intakes, C-Reactive Protein, and the Metabolic Syndrome," *American Journal of Clinical Nutrition* 84(6) (2006): 1489-1497.

11. Tania Reyes-Izquierdo, Boris Nemzer, Ana Elizabeth Gonzalez, Qing Zhou, Ruby Argumedo, Cynthia Shu, and Zb Pietrzkowski, "Short-Term Intake of Calcium Fructoborate Improves WOMAC and McGill Scores and Beneficially Modulates Biomarkers Associated with Knee Ostoarthritis: A Pilot Clinical Double-blinded Placebo-controlled Study," *American Journal of Biomedical Sciences* 4(2) (2012): 111-122, doi:10.5099/aj120200111.

12. Romulus Ion Scorei, Paul Mitrut, Iulian Petrisor, and Iulia Daria Scorei, "A Double-Blind, Placebo-Controlled Pilot Study to Evaluate the Effect of Calcium Fructoborate on Systemic Inflammation and Dyslipidemia Markers for Middle-Aged People with Primary Osteoarthritis," *Biological Trace Element Research* 144(1-3) (2011): 253-263, doi:10.1007/s12011-011-9083-0.

13. Constantin Militaru, Ionut Donoiu, Alina Craciun, Iulia Daria Scorei, Anca Mihaela Bulearca, and Romulus Ion Scorei, "Oral Resveratrol and Calcium Fructoborate Supplementation in Subjects with Stable Angina Pectoris: Effects of Lipid Profiles, Inflammation Markers and Quality of Life," *Nutrition* 29(1) (2013): 178-83, doi:10.1016/j.nut.2012.07.006.

14. Ian R. Record, Ivor E. Dreosti, and Jennifer K, McInerney, "Changes in Plasma Antioxidant Status Following Consumption of Diets High or Low in Fruit and Vegetables or Following Dietary Supplementation with an Antioxidant Mixture," *British Journal of Nutrition* 85(4) (2001): 459-64, doi:10.1079/BJN2000292.

15. UNICEF and the Micronutrient Initiative, "Vitamin and Mineral Deficiency: A Global Progress Report," *The Micronutrient Initiative*, Ottawa (Canada), 2004, http://www.micronutrient.org/english/View.asp?x=614

16. Jayson B. Calton, "Prevalence of Micronutrient Deficiency in Popular Diet Plans," *Journal of the International Society of Sports Nutrition* 7(24) (2010), doi:10.1186/1550-2783-7-24.

17. Abay Asfaw, "Micronutrient Deficiency and the Prevalence of Mothers' Overweight/Obesity in Egypt," *Economics and Human Biology* 5(3) (2007): 471-483.

18. Kathleen M. Fairfield and Robert H. Fletcher, "Vitamins for Chronic Disease Prevention in Adults," *Journal of the American Medical Association* 287(23) (2002): 3116-3126, doi:10.1001/jama.287.23.3116.

CHAPTER 25

On the Subject of Taking Action

Michael E. Gerber

Deliberation is the work of many men. Action, of one alone.

—Charles de Gaulle

I t's time to get started, time to take action. Time to stop thinking about the old practice and start thinking about the new practice. It's not a matter of coming up with better practices; it's about reinventing the practice of healthcare.

And the healthcare practitioner has to take personal responsibility for it.

That's you.

So sit up and pay attention!

You, the healthcare practitioner, have to be interested. You cannot abdicate accountability for the practice of healthcare, the administration of healthcare, or the finance of healthcare.

Although the goal is to create systems into which healthcare practitioners can plug reasonably competent people—systems that allow the practice to run without them—healthcare practitioners must take responsibility for that happening.

I can hear the chorus now: "But we're healthcare practitioners! We shouldn't have to know about this." To that I say: whatever. If you don't give a flip about your practice, fine—close your mind to new knowledge and accountability. But if you want to succeed, then you'd better step up and take responsibility, and you'd better do it now.

All too often, healthcare practitioners take no responsibility for their business, but instead delegate tasks without any understanding of what it takes to do them; without any interest in what their people are actually doing; without any sense of what it feels like to be at the front desk when a patient comes in and has to wait for forty-five minutes; and without any appreciation for the entity that is creating their livelihood.

Practitioners can open the portals of change in an instant. All you have to do is say, "I don't want to do it that way anymore." Saying it will begin to set you free—even though you don't yet understand what the practice will look like after it's been reinvented.

This demands an intentional leap from the known into the unknown. It further demands that you live there—in the unknown— for a while. It means discarding the past, everything you once believed to be true.

Think of it as soaring rather than plunging.

Thought Control

You should now be clear about the need to organize your thoughts first, and then your business. Because the organization of your thoughts is the foundation for the organization of your business.

If we try to organize our business without organizing our thoughts, we will fail to attack the problem.

We have seen that organization is not simply time management. Nor is it people management. Nor is it tidying up desks or alphabetizing patient files. Organization is first, last, and always cleaning up the mess of our minds.

By learning how to *think* about the practice of healthcare, by learning how to *think* about your priorities, and by learning how to *think* about your life, you'll prepare yourself to do righteous battle with the forces of failure.

Right thinking leads to right action—and now is the time to take action. Because it is only through action that you can translate thoughts into movement in the real world, and, in the process, find fulfillment.

So, first *think* about what you want to do. Then *do* it. Only in this way will you be fulfilled.

How do you put the principles we've discussed in this book to work in your practice? To find out, accompany me down the path once more:

1. *Create a story about your practice.* Your story should be an idealized version of your practice, a vision of what the preeminent healthcare practitioner in your field should be and why. Your story must become the very heart of your practice. It must become the spirit that mobilizes it, as well as everyone who walks through the doors. Without this story, your practice will be reduced to plain work.

2. *Organize your practice so that it breathes life into your story.* Unless your practice can faithfully replicate your story in action, it all becomes fiction. In that case, you'd be better off not telling your story at all. And without a story, you'd be better off leaving your practice the way it is and just hoping for the best.

Here are some tips for organizing your practice:

- Identify the key functions of your practice.
- Identify the essential processes that link those functions.
- Identify the results you have determined your practice will produce.
- Clearly state in writing how each phase will work.

Take it step by step. Think of your practice as a program, a piece of software, a system. It is a collaboration, a collection of processes dynamically interacting with one another.

Of course, your practice is also people.

3. *Engage your people in the process.* Why is this the third step rather than the first? Because, contrary to the advice most business experts will give you, you must never engage your people in the process until you yourself are clear about what you intend to do.

The need for consensus is a disease of today's addled mind. It's a product of our troubled and confused times. When people don't know what to believe in, they often ask others to tell them. To ask is not to lead but to follow.

The prerequisite of sound leadership is first to know where you wish to go.

And so, "What do I want?" becomes the first question; not, "What do they want?" In your own practice, the vision must first be yours. To follow another's vision is to abdicate your personal accountability, your leadership role, your true power.

In short, the role of leader cannot be delegated or shared. And without leadership, no healthcare practice will ever succeed.

Despite what you have been told, win-win is a secondary step, not a primary one. The opposite of win-win is not necessarily they lose.

Let's say "they" can win by choosing a good horse. The best choice will not be made by consensus. "Guys, what horse do you think we should ride?" will always lead to endless and worthless discussions. By the time you're done jawing, the horse will have already left the post.

Before you talk to your people about what you intend to do in your practice and why you intend to do it, you need to reach agreement with yourself.

It's important to know (1) exactly what you want, (2) how you intend to proceed, (3) what's important to you and what isn't, and (4) what you want the practice to be and how you want it to get there.

Once you have that agreement, it's critical that you engage your people in a discussion about what you intend to do and why. Be clear—both with yourself and with them.

The Story

The story is paramount because it is your vision. Tell it with passion and conviction. Tell it with precision. Never hurry a great story. Unveil it slowly. Don't mumble or show embarrassment. Never apologize or display false modesty. Look your audience in the eyes and tell your story as though it is the most important one they'll ever hear about a practice. Your practice. The practice into which you intend to pour your heart, your soul, your intelligence, your imagination, your time, your money, and your sweaty persistence.

Get into the storytelling zone. Behave as though it means everything to you. Show no equivocation when telling your story.

These tips are important because you're going to tell your story over and over—to patients, to new and old employees, to healthcare practitioners, to associate healthcare practitioners, and to your family and friends. You're going to tell it at your church or synagogue, to your card-playing or fishing buddies, and to organizations such as Kiwanis, Rotary, YMCA, Hadassah, and Boy Scouts.

There are few moments in your life when telling a great story about a great practice is inappropriate.

If it is to be persuasive, you must love your story. Do you think Walt Disney loved his Disneyland story? Or Ray Kroc his McDonald's story? What about Dave Smith at Federal Express? Or Debbie Fields at Mrs. Field's Cookies? Or Tom Watson Jr. at IBM?

Do you think these people loved their stories? Do you think others loved (and *still* love) to hear them? I daresay *all* successful entrepreneurs have loved the story of their business. Because that's what true entrepreneurs do. They tell stories that come to life in the form of their business.

Remember: A great story never fails. A great story is always a joy to hear.

In summary, you first need to clarify, both for yourself and for your people, the *story* of your practice. Then you need to detail the *process* your practice must go through to make your story become reality.

I call this the business development process. Others call it reengineering, continuous improvement, reinventing your practice, or total quality management.

Whatever you call it, you must take three distinct steps to succeed:

- *Innovation.* Continue to find better ways of doing what you do.

- *Quantification.* Once that is achieved, quantify the impact of these improvements on your practice.

- *Orchestration.* Once these improvements are verified, orchestrate this better way of running your practice so that it becomes your standard, to be repeated time and again.

In this way, the system works—no matter who's using it. And you've built a practice that works consistently, predictably, systematically. A practice you can depend on to operate exactly as promised, every single time.

Your vision, your people, your process—all linked.

A superior practice is a creation of your imagination, a product of your mind. So fire it up and get started! Now let's discover what Dr. Hayes has to say about taking action. ✢

CHAPTER 26

Creating the Perfect Nutrition Profit Center

Dr. Donald L. Hayes, DC

Action may not always bring happiness, but there is no happiness without action.

—William James

I s it possible to have a perfect nutrition profit center? The concept certainly means different things to different healthcare practitioners. However, having spent over twenty years in practice and more than fifteen years consulting some of the most successful nutrition profit centers in the world, I have discovered some key components that, when applied together, can make the perfect nutrition profit center a reality for you.

Before I list my Top Ten Action Steps that make up a perfect nutrition profit center, it's important to understand that implementing any of these concepts into your practice requires a shift in your current way of thinking. The number one thing you have to be prepared to do is make changes. Michael told us just how long it takes to make a change in our lives when he said you can "open the portals of change in an instant." All we have to do is say, "I don't want to do it that way anymore." In other words, right thinking leads to right action. Let's start some right thinking in this chapter by observing some of the things most of us don't like about practice—things that make our practice less than perfect.

Things We Don't Like About Practice

Too many of us don't enjoy our time in practice; it's simply not as fun as it was when we first opened our doors. We're tired of working more and more hours year after year.

We really don't like the fact that we have to focus so much of our time on the money part of the practice; we would rather just treat patients and go home. Making money was not part of our thinking while in school, but now it seems to be front and center. We wish that somehow, money could be less of an issue.

We really don't enjoy the long hours that are required to operate our practice, forcing us to be away from our families. We really hate not having every weekend available to spend at home because we're doing some type of practice event instead.

We dislike the fact that, although we have employees on the payroll who cost us money, it seems like we still have to do way too much work ourselves in order to get anything done.

We realize we need new patients, but we really hate the idea of spending so much of our personal time doing various marketing events to get them. We wish there were some type of automated marketing system that could help bring new patient referrals into the office on a regular basis.

We know the value of educating patients about health, but we just wish there was a more systematic way of doing it that didn't involve so much of our own personal time.

Clearly, there's a lot we don't like. So let's shift gears and see what a perfect nutrition profit center might look like and how it might change the things we don't like.

My Top Ten Action Steps for the Perfect Nutrition Profit Center

Michael makes it sound so simple: "Think about what you want to do and then do it." With that in mind, here are my Top Ten Action Steps, the key components of the perfect nutrition profit center. Some I've discovered myself while in private practice, and others I've unearthed from my years of consulting some of the world's top doctors.

Action Step #1: Do Less, Not More

By now I'm sure you fully understand that in order to create a perfect nutrition profit center you'll need to put into place a set of E-Myth-based turnkey systems which will allow you to plug in other people (like associates and staff) who can follow the systems that run the routine portions of the nutrition profit center so you don't have to.

When the right systems are in place, your nutrition profit center will work no matter who operates it. You'll know you've built it correctly when you can count on it to operate the same way every single day, consistently, predictably, and systematically, whether you are in the office or not. When this is accomplished, you won't need to work more hours in a day or more days in a week. In fact, you'll now be able to work as much or as little as you want. Doing less instead of doing more is a significant step in the right direction towards a perfect nutrition profit center.

Action Step #2: Generate Ongoing, Effortless, Monthly Revenue

Every business must make money, and your nutrition profit center is no exception. The secret to making money in a healthcare practitioner's office today is to have a very high patient satisfaction rating. Patients should be so thrilled with your fees, your hours, your on-time schedule, your services, and your nutrition products that they remain patients for life. Because of their experience with your office, they end up telling everyone they know about you, without you ever having to ask them to do so. With the proper practice systems in place, you'll be able to make consistent money from your primary services while also generating a steady amount of residual income from your nutrition profit center profit center that basically runs itself.

Nutrition products with repeat sales generate ongoing, effortless, monthly revenues for your practice. In a very short amount of time, regular repeat monthly purchases of nutrition products by your new, active, and inactive patients can generate enough income to cover your practice expenses. Imagine starting the first working day of each month knowing that the nutrition profits for that month alone will pay your salary and all of your practice expenses. Suddenly, your financial stress evaporates.

You will exceed your patients' expectations when you focus on supporting their main complaint with a Whole Body Alkaline Nutrition support package. When your nutrition system can also help raise their pH, alkalize their body, quench free radicals, reduce inflammation, protect them against micronutrient deficiency, and provide them with a healthy weight management option, you continue to raise the bar on even the highest of patient expectations. And when patients get more than they expect, they'll tell others and they'll come back over and over again, generating ongoing revenue with almost no extra effort from you.

Action Step #3: Enjoy What You Do

With systems in place to run both your regular practice and your nutrition profit center, and trained staff to operate the systems so you don't have to, you have the opportunity to focus on the things you really enjoy; namely, spending more time with your patients.

You'll finally have the chance to be the healthcare practitioner you always wanted to be. You'll have the time to build long-term relationships with your patients, which is crucial to a successful referral-based practice. Spending a little extra time with each patient will make you stand out head and shoulders above your competition, and when your patients get to experience what that extra attention feels like, they'll want to share it with everyone they know, and the word will get out.

With systems in place, you'll be able to enjoy one other very important thing—staying on schedule. That means seeing patients at their appointed time! Wow, what a concept! Now your patients have bragging rights, and your day is so much more pleasant, free of the stress that comes from always being behind. Without a doubt, practice enjoyment is a huge part of a perfect nutrition profit center.

Action Step #4: Set Your Ideal Work Schedule

As much enjoyment as you'll get from working in your perfect nutrition profit center, you still need time off to recharge your life batteries. In fact, quality time away from your practice is a must for ensuring ongoing success. Your family needs you as much as your patients do, and you need time off with them to refresh your spirit. When you have a practice operating system in place that allows you to spend quality time with your family every week, you'll be able to arrive at your practice every Monday with renewed vigor.

In the perfect nutrition profit center, you need to establish a work schedule that includes quality time off. I suggest that you consider working four days straight and then take three days in a row off, every week. Plan to work full days Monday through Thursday and take every Friday, Saturday, and Sunday off.

This way, when you leave the office on Thursday, you can erase all practice related business from your mind until you return on Monday morning. This type of schedule will prevent you from burning out. It's the type of schedule you deserve, and you can enjoy it regardless of the size of your practice. If you break up the week any other way, you won't have the chance to get away and revitalize yourself; you need three full days in a row to do that. Try this schedule for a few weeks and you'll see how it can enrich your personal life, your family life, and your practice growth.

Because you have trained your staff (and possibly an associate) to follow the operating system, your office can still remain open five or six days a week to provide services and nutrition products to your patients, but you won't have to be there. Working just four days a week and getting three days off in a row, yet having your practice open to serve your community five to six days a week, is a dream come true and a major component of a perfect nutrition profit center.

Action Step #5: Attract New Patients with Ease

A guaranteed way to end your money problems once and for all is to have a steady stream of new patients coming into your practice each and every week without you or your staff having to do any extra work.

In the perfect nutrition profit center, you don't have to spend all of your free evenings and weekends marketing your practice. All you have to do is implement a proven turnkey marketing system that basically does the marketing work for you; one that stimulates new patients, improves compliance, and increases nutrition sales so you and your staff can focus on treating patients.

When the marketing system you put in place is generating new patient referrals and nutrition sales automatically, you're able to leave your office every Thursday free from worry because you have the certainty that new patients will walk through your office door each and every week.

Action Step #6: Stop Selling

When you operate a perfect nutrition profit center, you and your staff focus on giving patients exactly what they need, not selling them a bunch of vitamins. Patients want to feel better as soon as possible, and when you offer them a Whole Body Alkaline Nutrition system that supports their health goals by raising internal pH and helping to quickly reduce inflammation, you'll be rewarded with long-term relationships, endless new patient referrals, and an outrageously successful practice. When patients stick around long term, it gives you and your staff a chance to educate them on wellness.

Action Step #7: Systematize Patient Education

When you systematize the patient education process, you're able to spend more clinic time with patients and more free time with your family. A lot of healthcare practitioners sacrifice their precious personal time conducting events to help educate patients on health. The perfect nutrition profit center accomplishes the educational process in a different way, by systematizing the internal, external, and internet marketing of your practice. This professional, methodical approach not only educates patients on the value of good health, it also helps to build long-term relationships, generate referrals, and substantially increase nutrition sales.

Action Step #8: Bring Back Inactive Patients

If I had to guess, I'd say you have three times more inactive patients than active patients. When you use an automated turnkey professional marketing system that educates and builds relationships, you can reactivate a majority of your inactive patients. This type of system provides an extremely inexpensive way to reinvigorate previous patients, stimulate new patient referrals, pull in existing patients more frequently, and increase nutrition product sales. The perfect nutrition profit center constantly strives to reactivate all inactive patients.

Action Step #9: Expand Your Reach with a No Inventory Online Nutrition Store

Every patient you treat has family and friends who are not patients who live in town, and many more who live out of town. It's important for you and your staff to realize that you have influence over all of them. Those that live in town may feel they don't need your clinical services now, while those that live out of town are simply too far away to ever visit your practice. By promoting your No Inventory Online Nutrition Store to all your active patients and encouraging them to welcome their friends and relatives to visit it and purchase products (even if those people are not active patients themselves), you can boost your profits and give your perfect nutrition profit center a world-wide reach.

Action Step #10: Build Long-Term Practice Relationships

Healthcare practitioners today are ceaselessly debating the best way to build a lucrative practice. I know from experience that the most successful way is to create and maintain long-term relationships. Systematized patient education, coupled with an automated online nutrition store, will help you focus on just that by inviting patients to stay with you for life. And as these relationships deepen and multiply, patients help to build the practice not only through their individual participation, but also through their regular referrals of family, co-workers, and friends. In order to achieve the perfect nutrition profit center, you must spend all your effort and resources on developing and nurturing these relationships.

Take Action

Synthesize these Ten Action Steps and then get out there and do them! Transform your secondary profit center into a Perfect Nutrition

Profit Center. Let your imagination run wild and strive to create a superior, efficient, and enjoyable business. Take right action from a place of passionate engagement with your staff, your associates, and most importantly, your patients, and you cannot go wrong. Make your nutrition profit center work for you and create the life you've always dreamed! ✤

AFTERWORD

Michael E. Gerber

For more than three decades, I've applied the E-Myth principles I've shared with you here to the successful development of thousands of small businesses throughout the world. Many have been healthcare practice – from small-town offices to large wellness centers, with healthcare practitioners from every specialty.

Few rewards are greater than seeing these E-Myth principles improve the work and lives of so many people. Those rewards include seeing these changes:

- Lack of clarity—clarified.
- Lack of organization—organized.
- Lack of direction—shaped into a path that is clearly, lovingly, passionately pursued.
- Lack of money or money poorly managed—money understood instead of coveted; created instead of chased; wisely spent or invested instead of squandered.
- Lack of committed people—transformed into a cohesive community working in harmony toward a common goal; discovering one another and themselves in the process; all the while expanding their understanding, their know-how, their interest, their attention.

After working with so many healthcare practitioners, I know that a practice can be much more than what most become. I also know that nothing is preventing you from making your practice all that it can be. It takes only desire and the perseverance to see it through.

In this book—the next of its kind in the E-Myth Expert series—the E-Myth principles have been complemented and enriched by stories from Dr. Hayes, a real-life healthcare practitioner and expert in the field of nutrition who has helped hundreds of providers put these principles to use in their practice. Many of those healthcare practitioners have had the desire and perseverance to achieve success beyond their wildest dreams. Now you, too, can join their ranks.

I hope this book has helped you clear your vision and set your sights on a very bright future.

To your practice and your life, good growing!

ABOUT THE AUTHOR

Michael E. Gerber

Michael E. Gerber is the international legend, author, and thought leader behind the E-Myth series of books, including *The E-Myth Revisited*, *E-Myth Mastery*, *The E-Myth Manager*, *The E-Myth Enterprise*, *The Most Successful Small Business in the World and Awakening the Entrepreneur Within*. Collectively, Mr. Gerber's books have sold millions of copies worldwide. Michael Gerber is the founder of Michael E. Gerber Companies, E-Myth Worldwide, The Dreaming Room™, and his newest venture, Design, Build, Launch & Grow™. Since 1977, Mr. Gerber's companies have served the business development needs of over 70,000 business clients in over 145 countries. Regarded by his avid followers as the thought leader of entrepreneurship worldwide, Mr. Gerber has been called by Inc. Magazine, "the world's #1 small business guru." A highly sought-after speaker and strategist, who has single handedly been accountable for the transformation of small business worldwide, Michael lives with his wife, Luz Delia, in Carlsbad, California.

ABOUT THE CO-AUTHOR

Dr. Donald L. Hayes, DC

Donald L. Hayes, DC is President and Owner of Wellness Watchers Global, LLC and Ceautamed Worldwide, LLC, the makers of the Greens First nutrition product line.

Dr. Hayes received his Bachelor of Science from the University of Oregon, and his Doctorate in Chiropractic from Western States Chiropractic College in 1977. Dr. Hayes was in private practice for over twenty years. Throughout his career, Dr. Hayes has excelled as a clinician, educator, and author.

Dr. Hayes has formulated nutritional products that are offered by healthcare practitioners throughout the world. He has developed educational training programs for healthcare practitioners in the fields of nutrition, alternative and complementary medicine. He designed and delivered post-graduate nutrition education programs based on the E-Myth system to nearly 1,200 chiropractors, medical doctors, acupuncturists, naturopaths and their staff throughout the United States, Australia and New Zealand.

Dr. Hayes credits the use of the E-Myth system in all of his business ventures as the foundation for their success. He teaches healthcare practitioners how to use the E-Myth Principals to effectively offer nutrition in their practice.

Dr. Hayes is the author of a number of popular nutrition books including *Alkalize Now—The pH Balance Program, The 7 Habits of Healthy Living, The 90-Day Food & Exercise Diary,* and *Re-juve-nation: A 3-Week Alkalizing, Joint Health & Detoxification Program.*

Dr. Hayes lectures nationally and internationally to doctors, corporations, and public groups on the subjects of applied nutrition, functional medicine, wellness, and anti-aging strategies. His vision inspires others to a better quality of life for themselves and their families.

ABOUT THE SERIES

The E-Myth Expert series brings Michael E. Gerber's proven E-Myth philosophy to a wide variety of different professional business areas. The E-Myth, short for "Entrepreneurial Myth," is simple: Too many small businesses fail to grow because their leaders think like technicians, not entrepreneurs. Gerber's approach gives small enterprise leaders practical, proven methods that have already helped transform tens of thousands of businesses. Let the E-Myth Expert series boost your professional business today!

Books in the series include:

The E-Myth Attorney
The E-Myth Accountant
The E-Myth Optometrist
The E-Myth Chiropractor
The E-Myth Financial Advisor
The E-Myth Landscape Contractor
The E-Myth Architect
The E-Myth Real Estate Brokerage
The E-Myth Insurance Store
The E-Myth Real Estate Investor
The E-Myth Dentist
The E-Myth Nutritionist

Forthcoming books in the series include:

The E-Myth Bookkeeper
The E-Myth Veterinarian
. . . and 300 more industries and professions

Learn more at: www.michaelegerber.com/co-author

Have you created an E-Myth enterprise? Would you like to become a co-author of an E-Myth book in your industry? Go to www.michaelegerber.com/co-author.

THE MICHAEL E. GERBER
ENTREPRENEUR'S LIBRARY
It Keeps Growing . . .

Thank you for reading another E-Myth Vertical book.

Who do you know who is an expert in their industry?

Who has applied the E-Myth to the improvement of their
practice as Dr. Donald L. Hayes, DC has?

Who can add immense value to others in his or her industry
by sharing what he or she has learned?

Please share this book with that individual and share that individual with us.

We at Michael E. Gerber Companies are determined to transform the state
of small business and entrepreneurship worldwide. *You can help*.

To find out more, email us at Michael E. Gerber Partners, at
gerber@michaelegerber.com.

To find out how YOU can apply the E-Myth to YOUR practice,
contact us at gerber@michaelegerber.com.

Thank you for living your Dream, and changing the world.

Authors of Business Design

Michael E. Gerber, Co-Founder/Chairman
Michael E. Gerber Companies™
Creator of The E-Myth Evolution™
P.O. Box 131195, Carlsbad, CA 92013
760-752-1812 O • 760-752-9926 F
gerber@michaelegerber.com
www.michaelegerber.com

Join The Evolution ^{SM}

Attend the Dreaming Room™ Trainings
www.michaelegerber.com/dreaming-room

Awaken the Entrepreneur Within You
www.michaelegerber.com/facilitator-training

Michael E. Gerber Partners
www.michaelegerber.com/are-you-the-one

Listen to the Michael E. Gerber Radio Show
www.blogtalkradio.com/michaelegerber

Watch the latest videos
www.youtube.com/michaelegerber

Connect on LinkedIn
www.linkedin.com/in/michaelegerber

Connect on Facebook
www.facebook.com/MichaelEGerberCo

Follow on Twitter
http://twitter.com/michaelegerber

CPSIA information can be obtained at www.ICGtesting.com
Printed in the USA
BVOW07*0711171114

374758BV00011B/20/P